REVELATION
the End

ALYSA VANDERWEERD

. . . .

....

IN HIS PRESENCE *series*

Redeeming the Time: Psalm 16:11
Radical Living: the Book of James
the End: the Book of Revelation

INTRODUCTION

Jesus is returning! Does that excite you or freak you out?

Personally, I get excited. But it's because I've studied the book of Revelation and the truth of God's word eases minds. There is no fear for the Christian in end times. Why? Because the revelation of Jesus Christ assures victory for the Christian – the book of Revelation is a promise of rescue! Jesus Christ is the Beginning and the End. Rest assured, the end is good for the believer. For every good and perfect gift comes from the Father of lights — **James 1:17**, and Jesus Christ is the greatest gift — **2 Corinthians 9:15**. Just give me Jesus!

The non-believer, however, has every right to fear. Do you care whether your friends know Jesus or not? See, here is the thing, friends don't let friends die without Jesus. Hearts should be rejoicing with those who rejoice in the Lord, and they should be weeping for those who refuse to accept Him as their Savior — **Romans 12:15**. God has commanded us to go into all the world and preach the gospel — **Mark 16:15**; the best and sometimes the most hardest place to start is with those that you are close to. But believe me, as you go through this study, your heart will be triggered to reach out to the lost. Any person in their right mind would not want people to face the coming judgment. Nothing can stop this judgment from taking place – sin entered the world and God's holiness demands that it get dealt with. God in His love has given us a warning and He says "the time is near" — **Revelation 1:3**. But know this, the Giver of Good gifts promises to bless you for reading, listening, and obeying the words found in Revelation. Seriously – it's worth it!

I was freaked out back in 2012, when I realized I was going to be writing the curriculum for the Jr. High ministry at Harvest on Revelation. Not going to lie. I'm not sure if I was outwardly shaking when the pastor said, "Why don't we go through Revelation as our next book in the ministry?" But my heart was quaking. As a counselor, I, along with my friend simply asked the pastor for some book recommendations on Revelation. We wanted to learn. And that was his response. Go figure. But guess what? After studying this book, it literally became one of my favorite books in the bible. There is just something about it. I think you will realize it when you go through. Take my word for it – any time Jesus is revealed – it's worth it! Jesus clearly gives the difference between Himself and Satan when He says, "The thief does not come except to steal, and to kill, and to destroy. I have come that they may have life, and that they may have it more abundantly" –**John 10:10 NKJV**. Anytime Jesus is revealed a person witnesses the abundant life because Jesus Christ is life –**John 14:6**. He is the source of satisfaction from now through heaven's eternity!

Praying for all you who go through this study – that God illuminates His truths to you and gives you the eyes to see and the ears to hear what He is speaking to the church in the revelation of Jesus Christ.

Enjoy!

:: *Alysa VanderWeerd*

"The works of the LORD are great, studied by all who have pleasure in them. His work is honorable and glorious, and His righteousness endures forever. He has made His wonderful works to be remembered; the LORD is gracious and full of compassion."

Psalm 111:2-4 NKJV

....

MONDAY: WAKE UP

Is it hard for you to wake up? Do you hit the snooze button on your alarm FIVE times before you roll out of bed? Well, now is the time for you to —

"WAKE UP, for the coming of our salvation is nearer now than when we first believed." **Romans 13:11 NLT**.

Don't waste your life. Get to know God! Read His Word. Don't be caught sleeping when Jesus Christ returns. **WAKE UP** and prepare to meet Him.

How? Read the Bible to hear God's voice speaking to you. We don't just read the Bible for knowledge or information on what to do. We read the Bible to **know God**! To have a relationship with Him by knowing His heart, mind, and will for our lives, personally, and for the church. Here is how we can read God's Word to know Him better:

1.   **What does the verse say?[i]**

Example: **Isaiah 6:8 NLT "Then I heard the Lord asking, 'Whom should I send as a messenger to my people? Who will go for us?' And I said, 'Lord, I'll go! Send me.'"**

2.   **What is the lesson?**

Ask yourself: What is God doing or saying? Why is this important to God? Is God providing me with an example to follow? What is God calling me to obey Him in? Is there a promise in this verse that God is calling me to believe? Is God correcting my mindset and pointing me to His words of truth? Is God warning me that if I continue in a specific direction, I will stumble others or myself?

Example: **God is constantly searching for someone who is willing to serve Him and further His Kingdom here on earth.**

3.   **What is God telling you?**

....

How is God calling you to live out your faith? **James 1:22 NLT** says, "Don't just listen to God's word. You must do what it says. Otherwise you are only fooling yourselves." When you rephrase your lesson into a question, it becomes personal. God speaks in this, as your ears are opened to His direction.

Example: **Are you willing to serve God? Will you go where He tells you to go? Will you do what He calls you to do, no matter what?**

1. **What is your commitment?**

What did God speak to your heart? How did you answer the question? You can't live out this truth without the filling of the Holy Spirit. The world promotes self-efficacy — "I can do this on my own" — but as Christians we live God-dependent lives, knowing how much we need Him. Ask God to fill you with His Holy Spirit and make a commitment to live out this truth. On Fridays, write down if you kept your commitment. The Lord will give you the strength, as you seek Him. **Philippians 4:13** says, "I can do all things through Christ who strengthens me."

Example: **Isaiah 6:8- God wants me to willingly go where He tells me to go, serving Him in whatever capacity He calls me to. Like Isaiah, I say, "Lord, I'll go! Send me."** —7/14/12.

Before you start reading, pray! You can pray a prayer like this one: "Lord, please open my eyes to Your heart. Illuminate Your truths to me. Speak Lord, Your servant listens.

. . . .

TUESDAY: WORSHIP

After WAKING UP, it's time to WORSHIP...

"But the hour is coming, and is now here, when the true worshippers will WORSHIP the Father in spirit and truth, for the Father is seeking such people to worship him." **John 4:23 ESV**

Look around you, do you see true worshippers? True worshippers know God and surrender their life to Him — **John 4:22**. They worship Him by serving Him with gladness; coming before His presence, singing with joy — **Psalm 100:2**. They have a heart that is right before Him, desiring to honor Him with their life.

God the Father is seeking people who will worship Him in spirit; seeing the Invisible that will become visible upon heaven's entry—**1 Timothy 1:17**. This side of heaven, we walk by faith with a goal to please Him, knowing our faith will be made sight at His perfect time —**2 Corinthians 5:7-10**. "For God is Spirit, so those who worship him must worship in spirit and in truth"— **John 4:24 NLT**. So you see, when we worship in spirit, we envision God on the throne, as we are at His feet in adoration—**Revelation 4:10-11**. We believe what God has told us and, thus, worship before Majestic Glory.

God is also seeking people who will worship Him in truth. Truth is reality. It is what is right before our eyes. Truth can never be changed; it stands the test of time—**Proverbs 12:19**. Truth is absolute. The Word of God is truth. It is a sure foundation. Everlasting. Strong and steadfast. God's Word will never change—**John 1:14, Hebrews 13:8**. He has explained how to have right worship. Our worship is to be aligned with His Word in truth.

On Tuesday, we will read some historic hymns and will answer questions pertaining to them. In your group, look up the hymn and listen to it. Does the music enhance the written lyrics?

. . . .

WEDNESDAY: WAIT

After WAKING UP, WORSHIPPING, it's time to WAIT upon the Lord…

> "But those who WAIT on the LORD shall renew their strength; they shall mount up with wings like eagles, they shall run and not be weary, they shall walk and not faint." **Isaiah 40:31 NKJV**

When we wait upon the Lord, patiently persevering in prayer, our strength is increased as our faith grows. God will never leave us hanging; but there are times He calls us to press in, praying relentlessly, as we wait for Him to answer. It's not the time to give up praying; it is the time to wait upon Him—listening.

God speaks clearly in His Word. His Word will never change—**Hebrews 13:8**. No prayer has the power to change what God has set in stone. Prayer is not a way to manipulate God to do what we want Him to do; it is aligning our will with His established will found in His Word, asking for His will to be done on earth. It is a two-way conversation with our Father in heaven. He loves you and He wants you to seek Him and talk to Him, listening to Him—

. . . .

Jeremiah 29:13, Psalm 27:8.

When we approach God, we approach His throne of grace — **Hebrews 4:16**, assured of His glad welcome because of Jesus Christ's death on the cross and His resurrection — **Ephesians 3:12**. It is not by our merit that we approach Him, for we have all fallen short of the glory of God — **Romans 3:23**. Jesus' blood, however, shed on the cross atoned our sin; we are forgiven and welcomed in, as we repent and turn to Him — **Hebrews 9:22**.

Right now, there is a spiritual battle taking place that is unseen, but felt. People are going through various trials because the enemy is like a roaring lion seeking people to destroy — **1 Peter 5:8**. Satan wants people far from God, not moving in their giftings. Therefore, we resist the enemy, steadfast in the faith when we pray; drawing close to God — **1 Peter 5:9**. When we intercede on behalf of others we step into the battle, armed to fight the unseen. This war calls for spirit-filled weapons, not manmade — **2 Corinthians 10:4**. People will experience deliverance when we pray for God's will to be done; as God's will is stronger than Satan's — **Romans 8:38-39**.

God invites us to participate in establishing His will on earth. It's the call to be sensitive to His voice. He is searching for those loyal to Him, ready to show Himself strong on their behalf — **2 Chronicles 16:9**. Like Isaiah, do you hear Him calling out, "Who will go for Us?" Will you say, "Here I am Lord, send me" — **Isaiah 6:8**?

It is important to pray every day because as we pray we deepen our relationship with the Lord. For this study, we are also going to set aside a specific day to pray Scripture, interceding for our family, friends, community group, church, nation, leaders, and ourselves.

When Jesus taught His disciples to pray, He taught them the importance of honoring God's holy name, asking for His Kingdom to come soon and His will to be done on earth, petitioning for our needs, asking for forgiveness of our sins, deliverance from temptations and rescue from the evil one — **Matthew 6:9-13**. This helps us with right focus, reminding us of God's Sovereignty and reign in our lives. He is in control of everything! We approach Him in awe and reverence with thankful hearts.

For example:

READ: Revelation 1:3
Pray for your:

Family:

_____

_____

Friends:

_____

_____

Community Group:

_____

_____

Church:

_____

_____

Nation:

_____

_____

Leaders:

_____

_____

Yourself:

_____

_____

. . . . *the End* . . . .

THURSDAY: WORK

After WAKING UP, WORSHIPPING the Lord, and WAITING upon the Lord, it's time to WORK. . .

. . . .

"WORK hard so God can approve you. Be a good worker, one who does not need to be ashamed and who correctly explains the word of truth."
2 Timothy 2:15 NLT

It is really important to study God's truths to know Him. When you read God's Word and study it, you grow in your relationship with Him. This relationship anchors you, as you walk through life reaching out to others with the love of Jesus Christ. When you read God's truths, you are filled to overflowing, and it literally spills out onto everyone around you. You get to a point where you just can't hold back, it's like fire burning in your bones; you have to share Jesus — **Jeremiah 20:9**.

Jesus told us that the world will hate us — **John 15:19**. It's a fact. We will face various trials in this life. Who knows what kind or how heavy? We don't know the future, but God does; and He calls us to trust Him. He will keep us in perfect peace, as our minds are focused on Him, trusting Him — **Isaiah 26:3**. So, "trust in the LORD forever, for in YAH, the LORD, is everlasting strength" — **Isaiah 26:4 NKJV**. He has given us His word filled with promises, encouragement, corrections, warnings, commands — He's given us Jesus; everything we need to live a life of trust.

We need to work hard, studying God's Word; so that when we talk with others, or use our gifts for God's honor and glory, we are prepared. There are many who need to hear what God spoke to you. The word on your heart — the current word. You won't be prepared, if you don't take the time to study. What's important to you? You set aside time for that, right? Is your relationship with God important to you?

1 Peter 3:15-16 says, "If someone asks about your Christian hope, always be ready to explain it. But do this in a gentle and respectful way. Keep your conscience clear. Then if people speak against you, they will be ashamed when they see what a good life you live because you belong to Christ."

On Thursdays, you will read through a devotion and will search the Bible to answer the questions; growing in the grace and knowledge of your Lord and Savior Jesus Christ — **2 Peter 3:18**.

. . . .

FRIDAY: WITNESS

After WAKING UP, WORSHIPPING the Lord, WAITING upon the

. . . .

Lord, and WORKING, it's time to WITNESS!

"But you shall receive power when the Holy Spirit has come upon you; and you shall be WITNESSES to Me...to the end of the earth." **Acts 1:8 NKJV**

When we read through the book of Revelation, we realize we have nothing to fear. Victory is assured. Jesus Christ is returning for His own. We can live out our faith with confidence in our Lord and Savior. We are safe and secure. But are others? How about your friends that don't know Jesus. How will they encounter Him if you don't say anything?

James exhorts in **1:22 NLT**, "Don't just listen to God's word. You must do what it says. Otherwise, you are only fooling yourselves." This life is worth nothing if we don't practice what we preach. We would have a saved soul and a lost life. The adventure truly begins when we apply His word to our life; living out these truths in the everyday.

We can't do this on our own, though; so the Lord has given us the Holy Spirit to empower us to do His will. We are witnesses of the truth, pointing people to Jesus Christ. When we live God's word, people encounter Jesus; as we are His hands and feet in the lives of others. We truly are the pure tools, living clean lives, ready for the Master to use for a good work—**2 Timothy 2:21**. Your obedience to God's commands in taking steps of faith, perfects your faith – making it complete—**James 2:22**.

On Fridays, we are going to live out what we learned this past week, putting our faith into action.

....

REVELATION
the End

. . . .

Week 1: Revelation 1:1-3

MONDAY: WAKE UP

"WAKE UP, for the coming of our salvation is nearer now than when we first believed." **Romans 13:11 NLT**

Lord, please open my eyes to Your heart. Illuminate Your truths to me.

Speak Lord, Your servant listens.

Read: **Revelation 1:1-3**

What does the verse say?

_____
_____
_____
_____
_____
_____

What is the lesson?

_____
_____
_____
_____
_____
_____

What is God telling you?

_____
_____
_____
_____
_____
_____

REVELATION
the End

What is your commitment?

_____

_____

_____

_____

_____

_____

. . . .

TUESDAY: WORSHIP

After WAKING UP, it's time to WORSHIP…

"But the hour is coming, and is now here, when the true worshippers will WORSHIP the Father in spirit and truth, for the Father is seeking such people to worship him." **John 4:23 ESV**

Amazing Grace
John Newton, 1779

Amazing Grace, how sweet the sound,
That saved a wretch like me…
I once was lost but now am found,
Was blind, but now, I see.

T'was Grace that taught…
My heart to fear.
And Grace, my fears relieved.
How precious did that Grace appear…
The hour I first believed.

Through many dangers, toils and snares…
We have already come.
T'was Grace that brought us safe thus far…
And Grace will lead us home.

The Lord has promised good to me…
His word my hope secures.
He will my shield and portion be…
As long as life endures.
When we've been here ten thousand years…
Bright shining as the sun.
We've no less days to sing God's praise…
Then when we've first begun.

Amazing Grace, how sweet the sound,
That saved a wretch like me…

…………

I once was lost but now am found,
Was blind, but now, I see.

Read **John 1:14.** Jesus Christ is Grace! Reread this hymn and say "Jesus" instead of "Grace." What is this hymn saying?

_____
_____
_____
_____
_____
_____

The hymn says, "The Lord has promised good to me, His word my hope secures." What "good" does God promise in **Revelation 1:3**?

_____
_____
_____
_____
_____
_____

"He will my shield and portion be, as long as life endures." How is Jesus Christ our Shield? Read **Proverbs 30:5.**

_____
_____
_____
_____
_____

"We've no less days to sing God's praise, then when we've first begun." Read **Revelation 22:3.** If we are going to be constantly praising and worshiping God in heaven, what should we be doing while we are here on earth? Why?

_____
_____
_____
_____

. . . .

"But I know this: I was blind, and now I can see" — **John 9:25 NLT**. When did God open your eyes to your need for a personal relationship with Jesus Christ? Share your testimony.

_____
_____
_____
_____
_____
_____

PRAYER: Father, thank you for allowing me the privilege of worshiping

You in spirit and in truth!

WEDNESDAY: WAIT

After WAKING UP, WORSHIPPING, it's time to WAIT upon the Lord…

> "But those who WAIT on the LORD shall renew their strength; they shall mount up with wings like eagles, they shall run and not be weary, they shall walk and not faint." **Isaiah 40:31 NKJV**

READ: **Proverbs 20:12**
Pray for your:

Family:

_____
_____
_____
_____
_____
_____

Friends:

_____
_____
_____
_____
_____
_____

Community Group:

_____
_____
_____
_____
_____
_____

. . . .

WEEK ONE

Church:

_____
_____
_____
_____
_____
_____
_____

Nation:

_____
_____
_____
_____
_____
_____
_____

Leaders:

_____
_____
_____
_____
_____
_____
_____

Yourself:

_____
_____
_____
_____
_____
_____
_____

. . . .

THURSDAY: WORK

After WAKING UP, WORSHIPPING the Lord, and WAITING upon the Lord, it's time to WORK...

"WORK hard so God can approve you. Be a good worker, one who does not need to be ashamed and who correctly explains the word of truth." **2 Timothy 2:15 NLT**

The Time is Near
Read: **Revelation 1:1-3**

For the Christian, the Book of Revelation is a message of hope and redemption! It illuminates Jesus Christ in His glory and majesty. There is a specific blessing for the person who reads this book, listens, and obeys what it says. Do you want to be blessed?

The Book of Revelation reveals truth. It reveals Jesus Christ, who is Truth — **John 14:6**. It is a book for God's people, as God the Father gave it to His Son, Jesus Christ, who then gave it to His servants — **Revelation 1:1**. It's a promise to God's people, of what's to come — victory over evil! But if you do not acknowledge Jesus Christ as Lord, you won't understand it. If you choose to reject Jesus Christ and His grace, this book warns you of the judgment that is coming your way. You have a choice. Choose life — **Deuteronomy 30:19**!

See, our sin separates us from God. We've fallen short of His glory — **Romans 3:23**. The Bible tells us we deserve death — **Romans 6:23**! But, if we recognize that Jesus humbled Himself and died on the cross for us, taking all of our sin upon Himself — **Romans 5:8-9**; if we repent of our sin — **Acts 3:19** and confess with our mouths that Jesus is Lord, believing in our hearts that God raised him from the dead — we are saved — **Romans 10:9**!

Have you done this? Is Jesus Christ your personal Lord and Savior? If you have never invited Jesus Christ into your life, and you would like to, you can pray a prayer like this one:

. . . .

Dear Lord Jesus, I know that I am a sinner. I believe You died on the cross for my sins and that you rose again from the dead. I repent of my sins. I confess You as my personal Lord and Savior. Please help me to follow You ever day of my life. Thank You for saving me. Thank You for loving me. In Jesus' name I pray, Amen.

If you just received Jesus Christ into your life as your personal Lord and Savior, welcome to the family! Now your eyes are opened and you will be able to see truth clearly. Praise God!

An angel was sent to give the book of Revelation to John — **Revelation 1:1**. When Jesus first came to earth as a baby, God sent angels to announce His arrival. Whom did the angels tell and what happened?

_____

_____

_____

_____

_____

_____

Angels are created by God to minister to Him and to do what He calls them to do. Read **Hebrews 1.** How is Jesus far superior to the angels?

_____

_____

_____

_____

_____

_____

Read **Philippians 2:5-11.** When Jesus first came, He came in humiliation. Explain what happened and what God did.

_____

_____

_____

_____

_____

_____

Read **Matthew 25:1-13.** What does this parable say about Jesus

. . . .

Christ's return and the importance of being ready for Him?

_____
_____
_____
_____
_____
_____
_____

Read **2 Peter 3:1-15.** What does Peter tell us about the last days?

_____
_____
_____
_____
_____
_____
_____

PRAYER: Lord! Thank You for giving us the Revelation of Jesus Christ.

. . . .

FRIDAY: WITNESS

After WAKING UP, WORSHIPPING the Lord, WAITING upon

the Lord, and WORKING, it's time to WITNESS!

"But you shall receive power when the Holy Spirit has come upon
you; and you shall be WITNESSES to Me...to the end of the earth."
Acts 1:8 NKJV

"John faithfully reported the word of God and the testimony of Jesus
Christ" — **Revelation 1:2 NLT**. God specifically chose John to write the
book of Revelation. John had a decision to make. Obey or disobey? He
obeyed God. Your decisions define your character. Have you been
faced with a character defining decision recently? Share.

_____
_____
_____
_____
_____
_____

Who are you going to "faithfully" share Jesus Christ with? Do it!

_____
_____
_____
_____
_____
_____

Read **Revelation 1:3** and **John 9:4.** Time slips by quickly. Do you
sense the urgency? What task has God assigned you to do, while there
is still time? Do it!

_____
_____
_____
_____
_____
_____

. . . .

REVELATION
the End

How has God blessed you? Share.

_____
_____
_____
_____
_____
_____

How can you be used by God to bless someone else? Do it and share!

_____
_____
_____
_____
_____
_____

Angels are all throughout the Book of Revelation. But did you know, that angels come and go here on earth also! Read **Hebrews 13:2.** What should you do, and why?

_____
_____
_____
_____
_____
_____

The Bible tells us that we do not know the day or the hour when Jesus Christ will return — **Matthew 24:36**. But we are to watch for the signs Jesus mentioned that indicate His imminent return — **Matthew 24:3-14**. Name one thing that has happened recently that reveals "the time is near."

_____
_____
_____
_____
_____
_____

PRAYER: Father, thank You for blessing me!

. . . .

Week 2: **Revelation 1:4-8**

. . . .

MONDAY: WAKE UP

"WAKE UP, for the coming of our salvation is nearer now than when we first believed." **Romans 13:11 NLT**

Lord, please open my eyes to Your heart. Illuminate Your truths to me.

Speak Lord, Your servant listens.

Read: **Revelation 1:4-8**

What does the verse say?

_____
_____
_____
_____
_____
_____

What is the lesson?

_____
_____
_____
_____
_____
_____

What is God telling you?

_____
_____
_____
_____
_____
_____

. . . .

What is your commitment?

_____

_____

_____

_____

_____

_____

. . . .

TUESDAY: WORSHIP

After WAKING UP, it's time to WORSHIP...

"But the hour is coming, and is now here, when the true worshippers will WORSHIP the Father in spirit and truth, for the Father is seeking such people to worship him." **John 4:23 ESV**

To God Be the Glory
Fanny J. Crosby, 1875

To God be the glory, great things He hath done,
So loved He the world that He gave us His Son,
Who yielded His life an atonement for sin,
And opened the life gate that all may go in.

Refrain:
Praise the Lord, praise the Lord, Let the earth hear His voice!
Praise the Lord, praise the Lord, Let the people rejoice!
O come to the Father thro' Jesus the Son,
And give Him the glory, great things He hath done.

O perfect redemption, the purchase of blood,
To every believer the promise of God;
The vilest offender who truly believes,
That moment from Jesus a pardon receives.

Great things He hath taught us, great things He hath done,
And great our rejoicing thro' Jesus the Son;
But purer, and higher, and greater will be
Our wonder, our transport, when Jesus we see.

To God be the glory, the victory is won;
Our praise to the Savior has only begun;
In heavens radiant splendor we'll join with the throng
And praise Him forever with jubilant song.

....

Write out **Galatians 1:4-5.**

_____
_____
_____
_____
_____
_____

Read **Revelation 1:5-6.** Why do we give God the glory?

_____
_____
_____
_____
_____
_____

Knowing what God has done for you, how are you going to worship Him and give Him glory today?

_____
_____
_____
_____
_____
_____

What is this hymn saying? Share it's meaning with someone today.

_____
_____
_____
_____
_____
_____

PRAYER: Father, thank You for sending Jesus Christ to die on the cross for my sins. To God be the glory!

WEDNESDAY: WAIT

After WAKING UP, WORSHIPPING, it's time to WAIT upon the Lord…

"But those who WAIT on the LORD shall renew their strength; they shall mount up with wings like eagles, they shall run and not be weary, they shall walk and not faint." **Isaiah 40:31 NKJV**

READ: **Galatians 1:3-5**
Pray for your:

Family:

_____
_____
_____
_____
_____
_____

Friends:

_____
_____
_____
_____
_____
_____

Community Group:

_____
_____
_____
_____
_____
_____

…………

REVELATION
the End

Church:

_____
_____
_____
_____
_____
_____

Nation:

_____
_____
_____
_____
_____
_____

Leaders:

_____
_____
_____
_____
_____
_____

Yourself:

_____
_____
_____
_____
_____
_____

. . . .

THURSDAY: WORK

After WAKING UP, WORSHIPPING the Lord, and WAITING upon the Lord, it's time to WORK...

"WORK hard so God can approve you. Be a good worker, one who does not need to be ashamed and who correctly explains the word of truth." **2 Timothy 2:15 NLT**

Be Ready!
Read: **Revelation 1:4-8**

John opens this letter to the seven churches of Asia with the words "Grace and peace" — **Revelation 1:4-5**. In a book speaking of coming judgment, God comforts His people with the promise of the blessings of grace and peace. We Christians, who are right with God, have nothing to fear regarding what's to come.

But God is a just God and sins must be dealt with. He is the Alpha and the Omega, so He knows everything — **Revelation 1:8**. And He says, "People who cover their sins will not prosper. But if they confess and forsake them, they will receive mercy" — **Proverbs 28:13 NLT**. There is judgment for sin. But mercy and grace for the repentant sinner! Recognize your own sin and shout, "God, be merciful to me a sinner" — **Luke 18:13 NKJV**. Then look to the cross and see God's grace as the blood of Christ purifies hearts from deeds that lead to death — **Revelation 1:5, Hebrews 9:14**. And then experience His peace — **John 14:27**. To God be the glory! He is the perfect redemption.

In the last days, many will have the form of godliness but will deny its power — **2 Timothy 3:5**. Is that you? Do you look good on the outside — you go to church, carry a bible — but your heart is far from God? Repent! Turn back to God. Jesus is returning!

God changes people. He moves profoundly in lives, taking out hearts of stone and replacing them with hearts of flesh — **Ezekiel 36:26**. Has God changed you? Today, are you walking closer to God, reflecting

His image, more than ever before—**2 Corinthians 3:18**? Has God changed the hearts of the people around you? God is in the business of changing lives for His glory. So, as His priests—**Revelation 1:6**, will you confess God before men—**Matthew 10:32-33**, being vessels used to reach the lost?

This is the call to be ready! Jesus Christ is coming back and every eye will see Him—**Revelation 1:7**. Judgment is coming for the lost. Do you care if they are ready? How will they know about Jesus unless someone tells them—**Romans 10:4**? Will you go?

Read **Revelation 1:4,** and **1:8.** How is God described? What does this mean? Read **Exodus 3:14.**

_____

_____

_____

_____

_____

_____

Read **Revelation 1:4 NKJV.** "And from the seven Spirits who are before His throne." Who is this? Read **Isaiah 11:2,** and **Zechariah 4:1-10.**

_____

_____

_____

_____

_____

_____

How is Jesus described in **Revelation 1:5?**

_____

_____

_____

_____

_____

_____

Read **Revelation 1:6** and **1 Peter 2:9-10.** What does God call us? Why?

. . . .

_____
_____
_____
_____
_____
_____
_____

Read **Revelation 1:7,** and **Matthew 16:27, 24:29-30.** What's going to happen?

_____
_____
_____
_____
_____
_____

Read **Luke 12:40** and **1 Thessalonians 5:2.** Why should we be ready?

_____
_____
_____
_____
_____
_____

Read **Revelation 1:7, 9:21** and **Genesis 3:8-10.** Why are people going to "weep" or "mourn" when they see Jesus?

_____
_____
_____
_____
_____
_____

PRAYER: Father, thank You for forgiving me of my sin!

. . . .

FRIDAY: WITNESS

After WAKING UP, WORSHIPPING the Lord, WAITING upon the Lord, and WORKING, it's time to WITNESS!

> "But you shall receive power when the Holy Spirit has come upon you; and you shall be WITNESSES to Me...to the end of the earth."
> **Acts 1:8 NKJV**

Read **2 Peter 3:14.** Knowing that we are living in the last days, what type of life should you be living? Explain.

_____
_____
_____
_____
_____
_____

Read **Titus 2:11-13.** What are you going to do to make sure you are living a godly life? Explain.

_____
_____
_____
_____
_____
_____

Read **2 Peter 3:3-4** and **Revelation 1:7.** When people ask you why you are studying the book of Revelation and question its relevancy to life or they start scoffing or denying the fact that Jesus Christ is coming back, what are you going to do and say? Explain and share a verse.

_____
_____
_____
_____
_____
_____

. . . .

What is going to happen to the people who refuse to repent of their sins? Share a verse.

_____
_____
_____
_____
_____
_____

Read **Matthew 28:19-20.** Share the gospel with someone today.

_____
_____
_____
_____
_____
_____

Pray for the friends or family members that you know, that do not know Jesus Christ as their Lord and Savior.

_____
_____
_____
_____
_____
_____

PRAYER: Father, thank You for preparing me for Jesus Christ's return! Give me boldness to share the gospel with the lost.

....

REVELATION
the End

. . . .

Week 3: Revelation 1:9-20

. . . .

MONDAY: WAKE UP

"WAKE UP, for the coming of our salvation is nearer now than when we first believed." **Romans 13:11 NLT**

Lord, please open my eyes to Your heart. Illuminate Your truths to me.

Speak Lord, Your servant listens.

Read: **Revelation 1:9-20**

What does the verse say?

_____
_____
_____
_____
_____
_____

What is the lesson?

_____
_____
_____
_____
_____
_____

What is God telling you?

_____
_____
_____
_____
_____

. . . .

What is your commitment?

_____

_____

_____

_____

_____

_____

. . . .

TUESDAY: WORSHIP

After WAKING UP, it's time to WORSHIP…

"But the hour is coming, and is now here, when the true worshippers will WORSHIP the Father in spirit and truth, for the Father is seeking such people to worship him." **John 4:23 ESV**

Turn Your Eyes Upon Jesus
Helen H. Lemmel, 1922

O soul, are you weary and troubled?
No light in the darkness you see?
There's light for a look at the Savior,
And life more abundant and free!

Refrain:
Turn your eyes upon Jesus,
Look full in His wonderful face,
And the things of earth will grow strangely dim
In the light of His glory and grace.

Through death into life everlasting
He passed, and we follow Him there;
O'er us sin no more hath dominion-
For more than conqu'rors we are!

His Word shall not fail you—He promised;
Believe Him, and all will be well:
Then go to a world that is dying,
His perfect salvation to tell!

"And his face was as bright as the sun in all its brilliance" — **Revelation 1:16b NLT**. In times of trouble, why does God call us to look to Jesus? Explain and share a verse.

_____

_____

…………

_____
_____
_____
_____
_____
_____

Why should we worship Jesus when we are struggling? Explain and share a verse.

_____
_____
_____
_____
_____
_____

Read **2 Corinthians 4:6.** What does this verse mean? How does it give you hope?

_____
_____
_____
_____
_____
_____

Do you understand God's word better when you are worshipping Him? Explain.

_____
_____
_____
_____
_____
_____

PRAYER: Father, thank You for sending Your Son to be a light in this dark world. Thank You for allowing me to see His glory!

. . . .

WEDNESDAY: WAIT

After WAKING UP, WORSHIPPING, it's time to WAIT upon the Lord…

"But those who WAIT on the LORD shall renew their strength; they shall mount up with wings like eagles, they shall run and not be weary, they shall walk and not faint." **Isaiah 40:31 NKJV**

READ: **Philippians 2:5-8**
Pray for your:

Family:

_____
_____
_____
_____
_____
_____

Friends:

_____
_____
_____
_____
_____
_____

Community Group:

_____
_____
_____
_____
_____
_____

…………

REVELATION
the End

Church:

_____
_____
_____
_____
_____
_____

Nation:

_____
_____
_____
_____
_____
_____

Leaders:

_____
_____
_____
_____
_____
_____

Yourself:

_____
_____
_____
_____
_____
_____

THURSDAY: WORK

After WAKING UP, WORSHIPPING the Lord, and WAITING

upon the Lord it's time to WORK...

"WORK hard so God can approve you. Be a good worker, one who
does not need to be ashamed and who correctly explains the word of
truth." **2 Timothy 2:15 NLT**

A Vision
Read: **Revelation 1:9-20**

John walked and talked with Jesus, when He came as a humble
servant to this earth—**Philippians 2:5-8**. John stood at the foot of the
cross, listening intently as Jesus spoke some of His last words to him
personally before dying an agonizing death—**John 19:25-27**. John
knew Jesus was God--**John 10:30**, and it changed the way he lived! He
lived and breathed Jesus, sharing Christ's love with others. And he
was persecuted because of it—**Revelation 1:9**. But that didn't stop
him! Do you know Jesus in that way? Does persecution stop you?

John was exiled to an island. He was removed from people, forced by
the Roman authorities to stop preaching the Word and speaking
about Jesus—**Revelation 1:9**. But John stood quietly, enduring the
affliction, knowing that it came by God's divine direction; even in
isolation, he remained in God's presence—**Revelation 1:10**. And it
was there that he heard a voice and received the vision of Christ's
glory—**Revelation 1:10-20**. There on the island, he received the
command to write the book of Revelation. Know this, if you want to
be used by God for His glory, people cannot stop God from using
you!

In humility, John recognized that he was not the only one suffering
for Christ – that others in the church were also patiently enduring
through trial and tribulation—**Revelation 1:9, 2:9-10**. They needed
hope! They needed to see the vision of Christ's glory![1] See, sometimes
the greatest fruit in our lives is born out of affliction. When we

....

ourselves are broken and on our knees, weak in the world's eyes and weak before Christians, God uses us in powerful ways to meet needs that otherwise would not be met.

So, this message is to the church. "Hope has a name and it's Jesus Christ!" His glory is reflected in the church. We are the bearers of light and Jesus is in our midst — **Revelation 1:12-13**! We are His bride! He laid down His life for us so that we would be found holy — **Ephesians 5:25-27**. We have nothing to fear — **Revelation 1:17**. We may be broken vessels, but God chose us to house the precious treasure of the gospel, so that the lost world would be reached — **2 Corinthians 4:7**.

Christian! No weapon formed against you shall prosper — **Isaiah 54:17**. There's not much time left. Jesus is returning. So be bold! Share the gospel.

Read **Revelation 1:13**. Why is Jesus called "the Son of Man?" What does it mean? Read **Daniel 7:13; Matthew 16:27** (See also: **Matthew 19:28, 26:64; Revelation 1:7**).

_____
_____
_____
_____
_____
_____

Here in **Revelation 1:12-16**, we see a vision of Jesus Christ in His glory! How does John describe Him:

What do the seven gold lampstands represent? Read **Revelation 1:12, 20**.

_____
_____
_____
_____
_____
_____

Read **Revelation 1:13.** What does the full "garment" and gold band around his chest symbolize? Read **Exodus 28:4; Leviticus 16:4; Hebrews 4:14-15.**

_____

_____

_____

_____

_____

_____

Read **Revelation 1:14.** "His head and hair were white like wool." What does that mean? Read **Daniel 7:9, Isaiah 1:18; Ephesians 5:25-27; 1 Peter 1:15-16.**

_____

_____

_____

_____

_____

_____

Read **Revelation 1:14.** "His eyes were bright like flames of fire." What does that mean? Read **1 Corinthians 3:13-15; Hebrews 4:13.**

_____

_____

_____

_____

_____

Revelation 1:15. "His feet were as bright as bronze refined in a furnace." Read **Exodus 38:1-2.** What material was used on the altar? What does the altar in the Old Testament represent? Read **Psalm 110:1.** What does this verse say about the Lord's feet? Read **Hebrews 12:5-10.** What does God do?

_____

_____

_____

_____

_____

_____

. . . .

"His voice thundered like mighty ocean waves." What does that mean? Read **Ezekiel 1:24, 43:2; Hebrews 1:1-2.**

_____
_____
_____
_____
_____
_____

Revelation 1:16. "He held seven stars in his right hand." What do the "seven stars" represent? Read **Revelation 1:20, Luke 9:52.** What does "his right hand" represent? Explain.

_____
_____
_____
_____
_____
_____

"A sharp two-edged sword came from his mouth." What does that mean? Read **Hebrews 4:12.**

_____
_____
_____
_____
_____
_____

"And his face was as bright as the sun in all its brilliance." What does that mean? Read **Matthew 17:2; 2 Corinthians 4:6**

_____
_____
_____
_____
_____
_____

PRAYER: Thank You Lord for revealing Yourself to me!

. . . .

FRIDAY: WITNESS

After WAKING UP, WORSHIPPING the Lord, WAITING upon
the Lord, and WORKING, it's time to WITNESS!

> "But you shall receive power when the Holy Spirit has come upon
> you; and you shall be WITNESSES to Me...to the end of the earth."
> **Acts 1:8 NKJV**

Read **Revelation 1:9.** Have you ever felt isolated because of your
faithful witness of Jesus Christ? How did Jesus reveal Himself to you?

_____
_____
_____
_____
_____
_____

Do you know someone who stands alone in a certain situation, or
who is isolated from a group of people and feels hopeless? How can
you be Jesus' hands and feet in their life?

_____
_____
_____
_____
_____
_____

What are some different tactics the enemy has used against you to
keep you from sharing Jesus with others?

_____
_____
_____
_____
_____
_____

Read **Psalm 46:10.** Today, why do we fail to see Jesus moving in our

....

midst? Why do we not see His glory? Explain and share a verse.

_____
_____
_____
_____
_____
_____

When John saw Jesus in His glory, he fell down at His feet as if he were dead. But Jesus said, "Fear not!" — **Revelation 1:17** We know we are sinful people, how come we don't have to be afraid of being in God's presence? Explain and share a verse.

_____
_____
_____
_____
_____
_____

Read **2 Corinthians 5:20-21.** Knowing that Jesus Christ is coming back soon, what does God want you to do?

_____
_____
_____
_____
_____
_____

Read **Revelation 1:19-20** and **1 Corinthians 15:58.** What is your role in the church? How can you further God's Kingdom where He has placed you? (i.e: invite friends to church/community group, share the gospel with friends and family, help the poor, etc.)

_____
_____
_____
_____
_____
_____

Read **Revelation 1:11, 19.** In both verses, God told John to "write."

. . . .

What is God specifically calling you to do? Share.

_____

_____

_____

_____

_____

_____

PRAYER: Thank You Lord for using me, for Your glory, where You have placed me.

. . . .

REVELATION
the End

. . . .

Week 4: **Revelation 2:1-7**

. . . .

MONDAY: WAKE UP

"WAKE UP, for the coming of our salvation is nearer now than when we first believed." **Romans 13:11 NLT**

Lord, please open my eyes to Your heart. Illuminate Your truths to me.

Speak Lord, Your servant listens.

Read: **Revelation 2:1-7**

What does the verse say?

_____
_____
_____
_____
_____
_____

What is the lesson?

_____
_____
_____
_____
_____
_____

What is God telling you?

_____
_____
_____
_____
_____
_____

. . . .

What is your commitment?

_____

_____

_____

_____

_____

_____

. . . .

TUESDAY: WORSHIP

After WAKING UP, it's time to WORSHIP...

"But the hour is coming, and is now here, when the true worshippers will WORSHIP the Father in spirit and truth, for the Father is seeking such people to worship him." **John 4:23 ESV**

In the Garden
Charles A. Miles, 1913

I come to the garden alone,
While the dew is still on the roses,
And the voice I hear falling on my ear
The Son of God discloses.

And He walks with me, and He talks with me,
And He tells me I am His own;
And the joy we share as we tarry there,
None other has ever known.

He speaks, and the sound of His voice
Is so sweet the birds hush their singing,
And the melody that He gave to me
Within my heart is ringing.

I'd stay in the garden with Him,
Though the night around me be falling,
But He bids me go; through the voice of woe
His voice to me is calling.

Read **John 20:1-2, 11-16.** Do you long for Jesus with the same passion that Mary Magdalene had in the garden, when she couldn't find Him? Explain.

_____
_____
_____

....

_____
_____
_____

Read **John 20:15.** Name a time when you could not sense Jesus'
presence in your life? What did you do to draw near to Him? Explain.

_____
_____
_____
_____
_____
_____

Today, are you just going through the motions in your Christian life?
Or are you truly walking and talking with Jesus, hearing Him call you
His own? Explain.

_____
_____
_____
_____
_____
_____

This past week, have you worshipped Jesus more passionately? Why?

_____
_____
_____
_____
_____
_____

PRAYER: Father, thank You for sending Your Son, Jesus Christ, to die
on the cross for me! Thank You for giving me a Savior who knows my
name and wants to spend time with me.

. . . .

WEDNESDAY: WAIT

After WAKING UP, WORSHIPPING, it's time to WAIT upon the Lord...

> "But those who WAIT on the LORD shall renew their strength; they shall mount up with wings like eagles, they shall run and not be weary, they shall walk and not faint." **Isaiah 40:31 NKJV**

READ: **Matthew 22:37-39**
Pray for your:

Family:

_____
_____
_____
_____
_____
_____

Friends:

_____
_____
_____
_____
_____
_____

Community Group:

_____
_____
_____
_____
_____
_____

....

REVELATION
the End

Church:

_____
_____
_____
_____
_____
_____

Nation:

_____
_____
_____
_____
_____
_____

Leaders:

_____
_____
_____
_____
_____
_____

Yourself:

_____
_____
_____
_____
_____
_____

. . . .

THURSDAY: WORK

After WAKING UP, WORSHIPPING the Lord, and WAITING upon the Lord it's time to WORK...

"WORK hard so God can approve you. Be a good worker, one who does not need to be ashamed and who correctly explains the word of truth." **2 Timothy 2:15 NLT**

Change or be Chastened
Read: **Revelation 2:1-7**

Jesus loves His church! He built His church — **Matthew 16:18**. It is the place where God's glory is truly experienced. So, He guards it by confronting sin directly. In His love, Jesus gives His church an opportunity to repent and to be restored, or suffer the consequences for their rebellion. It is a word for us today as a church corporately, but also individually.

Here, Jesus writes to the church of Ephesus, reminding them that He is walking in their midst — **Revelation 2:1**, and that He sees everything that is going on in their church. He commends them for what they are doing right. "I know your works," Jesus says. "I know you work hard. I see you patiently enduring. I know you keep false teachers out, and that you hate the deeds of the Nicolaitans — **Revelation 2:2-3, 6**. With that, you are doing good. Nevertheless, I have this against you: you have left your first love — **Revelation 2:4 NKJV**."

Christian, are you praying as intensely as you used to or are your prayers heartless? Are you reading the Bible to hear God speak directly to your heart or are they just words on a page? Are you truly worshipping God or just singing the lyrics? Do you see Jesus or is your vision clouded with idols? Do you seek Jesus and His approval or the approval of man? Only you and Jesus can answer these questions. Jesus sees your heart — **Proverbs 21:2**. He knows your

....

motives — **Proverbs 20:27**. Do you love Jesus passionately or are you just going through the motions?

Have you left your first love? Then *remember* what it was like when you first accepted Jesus Christ as your Lord and Savior. What were you doing when you passionately loved Jesus? Next, *repent*. Stop sinning! Change directions. "Prove by the way that you live that you have really turned from your sins and turned to God" — **Matthew 3:8 NLT**. And finally, *return* and do the works you did at first.

Or else, Jesus will "remove your lampstand" — **Revelation 2:5**. Jesus will take away your light, your influence, your prominence. You will not be a city on a hill with your light shining for all to see — **Matthew 5:14**.

Today, the Lord is giving you a choice: change or be chastened! If your love for Jesus has grown cold, "God [will] use sorrow in [your] life to help [you] turn away from sin and seek salvation" — **2 Corinthians 7:10 NLT**. The sorrow can come in many forms; but it is designed specifically for you to directly hit your heart in order to wake you up and bring you to repentance. This sorrow will bring you to your knees in humble surrender, forcing you to seek Jesus passionately for His grace and mercy. You have a choice.

If you overcome, Jesus promises heaven and eternal life — **Revelation 2:7**. God gives grace to the repentant sinner. So, Christian, run to the cross! "May God's grace be upon all who love our Lord Jesus Christ with an undying love" — **Ephesians 6:24 NLT**. Let the glory of God's name be the passion of this church!

Read **Revelation 1:20, 2:1;** and **Hebrews 12:5-11.** Jesus is very involved in His church. What does He do in love? Explain.

_____
_____
_____
_____
_____
_____

Read **Matthew 22:37-38.** What is the greatest commandment?

_____

_____

_____

_____

_____

_____

Read **Revelation 2:2, 1 Thessalonians 5:20-22, 1 John 4:1-3,** and **Acts 17:10-11.** How does the church evaluate people, examine teaching, and exercise spiritual discernment? Why is this important?

_____

_____

_____

_____

_____

Read **1 John 5:21.** What draws your heart away from God? Explain.

_____

_____

_____

_____

_____

Read **Proverbs 4:23,** and **Matthew 6:33.** How do you guard your heart?

_____

_____

_____

_____

_____

Read **Revelation 2:5,** and **Matthew 3:8.** How do you demonstrate true repentance?

_____

_____

_____

_____

....

REVELATION
the End

_____
_____

Why is our love for Jesus Christ more important than our service for Him? Find a verse in the Bible to go with your answer.

_____
_____
_____
_____
_____
_____

PRAYER: Thank You Lord for loving me enough to discipline me when I don't put you first in my life.

. . . .

FRIDAY: WITNESS

After WAKING UP, WORSHIPPING the Lord, WAITING upon the Lord, and WORKING, it's time to WITNESS!

"But you shall receive power when the Holy Spirit has come upon you; and you shall be WITNESSES to Me...to the end of the earth."
Acts 1:8 NKJV

How are you doing spiritually? Have you left your first love? Explain.

_____
_____
_____
_____
_____
_____

Do you love someone or something more than Jesus? Explain.

_____
_____
_____
_____
_____
_____

Read **1 John 1:8-9.** What sins do you need to confess and repent of?

_____
_____
_____
_____
_____
_____

Read **Luke 22:54-62, John 21:15-17,** and **Ephesians 2:8.** Peter messed up! He denied Christ. But what did Jesus do?

_____
_____
_____

. . . .

REVELATION
the End

_____
_____
_____

What does this show you about your Lord and Savior and how does this apply to your life?

_____
_____
_____
_____
_____
_____

Your love for Jesus can fluctuate in intensity. What are you going to do to maintain your passion for Jesus Christ? Explain and share a verse.

_____
_____
_____
_____
_____
_____

With the people in your community group, figure out how you are going to be on "mission," igniting the hearts of each other with passion for Jesus and sharing the gospel in your schools. Do it and share what happened.

_____
_____
_____
_____
_____
_____

PRAYER: Father, thank You for never giving up on me! I love you!

....

Week 5: Revelation 2:8-11

....

MONDAY: WAKE UP

"WAKE UP, for the coming of our salvation is nearer now than when we first believed." **Romans 13:11 NLT**

Lord, please open my eyes to Your heart. Illuminate Your truths to me.

Speak Lord, Your servant listens.

Read: **Revelation 2:8-11**

What does the verse say?

_____
_____
_____
_____
_____
_____

What is the lesson?

_____
_____
_____
_____
_____
_____

What is God telling you?

_____
_____
_____
_____
_____
_____

....

REVELATION
the End

What is your commitment?

_____
_____
_____
_____
_____
_____
_____

. . . .

TUESDAY: WORSHIP

After WAKING UP, it's time to WORSHIP...

"But the hour is coming, and is now here, when the true worshippers will WORSHIP the Father in spirit and truth, for the Father is seeking such people to worship him." **John 4:23 ESV**

'Tis So Sweet To Trust In Jesus
Louisa M. R. Stead, 1882

'Tis so sweet to trust in Jesus,
Just to take Him at His Word;
Just to rest upon His promise,
And to know, "Thus saith the Lord!"

Jesus, Jesus, how I trust Him!
How I've proved Him o'er and o'er;
Jesus, Jesus, precious Jesus!
Oh, for grace to trust Him more!

Oh, how sweet to trust in Jesus,
Just to trust His cleansing blood;
And in simple faith to plunge me
'Neath the healing, cleansing flood!

Yes, 'tis sweet to trust in Jesus,
Just from sin and self to cease;
Just from Jesus simply taking
Life and rest, and joy and peace.

I'm so glad I learned to trust Thee
Precious Jesus, Savior, Friend;
And I know that Thou art with me,
Wilt be with me to the end.

Read **Proverbs 30:5**. How does this verse encourage you in worship?

....

_____
_____
_____
_____
_____
_____

Read **Psalm 84:11-12**. What promise does God make in these verses?

_____
_____
_____
_____
_____

Read **Isaiah 26:3-4**. Explain these verses.

_____
_____
_____
_____
_____

Read **Matthew 28:20**. What does Jesus promise?

_____
_____
_____
_____
_____

What does "trusting Jesus" look like? Share with a friend.

_____
_____
_____
_____
_____

PRAYER: Lord, thank You for walking with me through life's trials.

. . . .

WEDNESDAY: WAIT

After WAKING UP, WORSHIPPING, it's time to WAIT upon the Lord…

"But those who WAIT on the LORD shall renew their strength; they shall mount up with wings like eagles, they shall run and not be weary, they shall walk and not faint." **Isaiah 40:31 NKJV**

READ: **Isaiah 41:10**
Pray for your:

Family:

_____
_____
_____
_____
_____
_____

Friends:

_____
_____
_____
_____
_____
_____

Community Group:

_____
_____
_____
_____
_____
_____

…………

REVELATION
the End

Church:

_____
_____
_____
_____
_____
_____

Nation:

_____
_____
_____
_____
_____
_____

Leaders:

_____
_____
_____
_____
_____
_____

Yourself:

_____
_____
_____
_____
_____
_____

. . . .

THURSDAY: WORK

After WAKING UP, WORSHIPPING, it's time to WAIT upon the Lord!

"WORK hard so God can approve you. Be a good worker, one who does not need to be ashamed and who correctly explains the word of truth." **2 Timothy 2:15 NLT**

Don't Waste Your Pain!
Read: **Revelation 2:8-11**

"The Lord is my shepherd; I have everything I need" — **Psalm 23:1 NLT**. Jesus Christ is all you need! He is "the First and the Last, who died and is alive" — **Revelation 2:8 NLT**. He is God — **John 10:30**! Christian, when the world is against you, He upholds you. He is your source of strength.

Jesus writes this letter to the church in Smyrna. Suffering at the hands of persecutors because of their faithful witness of Jesus Christ, they needed encouragement. To this church, Jesus does not share one word of rebuke, only comfort. He knows His sheep — **John 10:27**, and He doesn't give them more than they can handle — **1 Corinthians 10:13**.

"I know about your suffering," He cries out — **Revelation 2:9**. Christian! Are you suffering? Then look up because Jesus is with you — **Matthew 28:20**. You are not alone. "Don't be afraid of what you are about to suffer," He continues — **Revelation 2:10 NLT**. Christian are you scared? Then cling to the promise that God has not given you a spirit of fear or timidity but of power, love, and a sound mind — **2 Timothy 1:7**.

This persecution you are facing is purifying you, purging you of sin, revealing your authenticity. A true Christian remains under the pressure of persecution, clinging to Christ for the rescue. A fake Christian runs — **1 John 2:19**. They can't handle the heat. They are not grounded on the Rock — **Matthew 7:24-27**. Christian, Jesus is calling out to you, "Remain faithful even when facing death, and I will give

....

REVELATION

the End

you the crown of life" — **Revelation 2:10 NLT**. Don't give up! There is an end to this trial. Keep praying — **Philippians 4:6-7**. The crown of life goes to people who have suffered and to those who have resisted temptation and have persevered under trial. There is a reward for your faithfulness and loyalty to the Lord! So, stay true to the Lord — **Acts 11:23**. Jesus is praying for you — **Hebrews 7:25**.

Christian, don't waste your pain! Comfort others with the comfort God has given you — **2 Corinthians 1:3-4**. People are watching you in your trial, as you bear up under the pressure, moving forward in faith. They see how your behavior far surpasses what a typical human is capable of. They see Jesus carrying you through! They see God's glory in your suffering. You are an example of God's faithfulness. He loves you! Share your story.

Read **Revelation 2:8** and **Psalm 27:1-6**. Why is it important to dwell in the house of the Lord?

_____
_____
_____
_____
_____
_____

Read **Luke 12:4-9**. Why should we fear God and not people?

_____
_____
_____
_____
_____
_____

Read **Psalm 34**. How does God divinely preserve His people when they are facing many afflictions and hardships?

_____
_____
_____
_____
_____

. . . .

Read **1 Peter 2:21-25**. How is Jesus an example to us in suffering?

_____

_____

_____

_____

_____

_____

Read **Galatians 5:22-26**. Why is it important to be filled with the Spirit—**Ephesians 5:18**, when facing adversity?

_____

_____

_____

_____

_____

_____

Read **2 Corinthians 12:7-10**. How is God's power displayed in your weakness?

_____

_____

_____

_____

_____

_____

Read **Revelation 2:11, 20:6**. What is the second death?

_____

_____

_____

_____

_____

_____

PRAYER: Father, thank You for comforting me in my trials.

. . . .

FRIDAY: WITNESS

After WAKING UP, WORSHIPPING the Lord, and WAITING upon the Lord it's time to WORK...

"But you shall receive power when the Holy Spirit has come upon you; and you shall be WITNESSES to Me...to the end of the earth."
Acts 1:8 NKJV

Are you facing a trial right now? Share.

_____
_____
_____
_____
_____
_____

How has Jesus drawn near to you in this trial?

_____
_____
_____
_____
_____
_____

Read **Romans 8:28-39**. How can you walk victoriously as a Christian when you are suffering?

_____
_____
_____
_____
_____
_____

Read **2 Corinthians 1:3-7**. Is a friend or family member facing something you have previously gone through? How can you comfort them with the comfort God has given you?

_____

. . . .

_____
_____
_____
_____
_____

Read **Romans 12:15**. When people around you are suffering, do you run away from them and their struggles or do you run to them ready to support them and pray for them?

_____
_____
_____
_____
_____

Has there been a time when God called you to do something for someone else (for example: pray for them, help them with something, listen to them), but you refused to do it? And then you noticed God used someone else to meet that need? God's will will always be done. Share a time when this happened and what you learned from that lesson.

_____
_____
_____
_____
_____

Are you, a friend, or a family member facing persecution because you are faithful to Jesus and what He has called you to do? Share.

_____
_____
_____
_____
_____

Read **Psalm 112:7**. Do you fear facing trials or persecution? Why?

_____

. . . .

_____
_____
_____
_____
_____
_____

Who is Polycarp? How does his testimony encourage you?

_____
_____
_____
_____
_____
_____

PRAYER: Father, thank You for giving me the strength to endure suffering. Your grace is sufficient for me!

. . . .

Week 6: **Revelation 2:12-17**

. . . .

MONDAY: WAKE UP

"WAKE UP, for the coming of our salvation is nearer now than when we first believed." **Romans 13:11 NLT**

Lord, please open my eyes to Your heart. Illuminate Your truths to me.

Speak Lord, Your servant listens.

Read: **Revelation 2:12-17**

What does the verse say?

_____
_____
_____
_____
_____
_____

What is the lesson?

_____
_____
_____
_____
_____
_____

What is God telling you?

_____
_____
_____
_____
_____
_____

. . . .

What is your commitment?

_____

_____

_____

_____

_____

_____

. . . .

TUESDAY: WORSHIP

After WAKING UP, it's time to WORSHIP...

"But the hour is coming, and is now here, when the true worshippers will WORSHIP the Father in spirit and truth, for the Father is seeking such people to worship him." **John 4:23 ESV**

Soldiers of Christ, Arise
Charles Wesley, 1749

Soldiers of Christ, arise
And put your armor on,
Strong in the strength which God supplies
Thro' His eternal Son;
Strong in the Lord of hosts
And in His mighty power.
Who in the strength of Jesus trusts
Is more than conqueror.

Stand then in His great might,
With all His strength endued.
And take, to arm you for the fight,
The panoply of God.
From strength to strength go on
And wrestle, fight and pray;
Tread all the powers of darkness down
And win the well-fought day.

Leave no unguarded place,
No weakness of the soul;
Take ev'ry virtue, ev'ry grace.
And fortify the whole;
That having all things done,
And all your conflicts past,
Ye may overcome thro' Christ alone
And stand complete at last.

....

Read **2 Timothy 2:3-4.** "Soldiers of Christ, arise." Explain this phrase.

_____
_____
_____
_____
_____
_____

Read **Revelation 2:17, 1 John 5:4** and **Romans 8:37.** How do Christians "overcome"?

_____
_____
_____
_____
_____
_____

Read **Ephesians 6:10-18.** As a soldier of Christ, how are you going to protect yourself from compromising with the world?

_____
_____
_____
_____
_____
_____

How does worship defeat the enemy? Share a verse.

_____
_____
_____
_____
_____
_____

PRAYER: Father, thank You for giving me victory in Jesus Christ!

. . . .

WEDNESDAY: WAIT

After WAKING UP, WORSHIPPING, it's time to WAIT upon the Lord…

"But those who WAIT on the LORD shall renew their strength; they shall mount up with wings like eagles, they shall run and not be weary, they shall walk and not faint." **Isaiah 40:31 NKJV**

READ: **Psalm 119:103-106**
Pray for your:

Family:

_____
_____
_____
_____
_____
_____

Friends:

_____
_____
_____
_____
_____
_____

Community Group:

_____
_____
_____
_____
_____
_____

…………

REVELATION
the End

Church:

_____
_____
_____
_____
_____
_____

Nation:

_____
_____
_____
_____
_____
_____

Leaders:

_____
_____
_____
_____
_____
_____

Yourself:

_____
_____
_____
_____
_____
_____

. . . .

THURSDAY: WORK

After WAKING UP, WORSHIPPING, it's time to WAIT upon the Lord!

"WORK hard so God can approve you. Be a good worker, one who does not need to be ashamed and who correctly explains the word of truth." **2 Timothy 2:15 NLT**

Will You Rock the Boat?
Read: **Revelation 2:12-17**

The Word of God cuts into a person's innermost thoughts and desires. It exposes us for who we really are — **Hebrews 4:12**. It draws us to repentance — **Acts 3:19** and reminds us of God's grace — **Ephesians 2:8-9**. The Word is powerful. It is alive!

Jesus applauds the church in Pergamum for their loyalty and faithfulness even though they lived in a city where the great throne of Satan was located — **Revelation 2:13**. Most of the believers in this church did hold fast to the truth; however, some believed false doctrine and the church allowed it — **Revelation 2:14-15, Numbers 22-25**. They did not confront sin. So, Jesus reminds them of the truth! You cannot compromise the truth to fit in with the world and think you are doing "ok" spiritually. It doesn't work that way.

In regards to religion, the world says, "What works for you is good and what works for me is good. All roads lead to heaven." But that is wrong! God says the road to heaven is narrow — **Matthew 7:13**. There is only one way to the Father in heaven and that is through Jesus Christ — **John 14:6**. There are moral absolutes. See, the world not only wants you to tolerate and accept what they believe, but they want you to approve of it also! They want you to compromise your faith. Today, are you compromising? Do you stand up for truth? Do you represent Jesus to an unrepentant world? Or do you try to live quietly and not "rock the boat"?

The church in Pergamum was compromising with the world and

....

Jesus called them to repentance! Jesus will protect His church while holding people responsible for their sins — **Revelation 2:16**. Today, do you need to repent?

After warning the church, Jesus encourages them with a couple blessings. To the person who overcomes they will receive hidden manna; which is Jesus Christ, our Living Bread — **John 6:51**. They will also receive a white stone. The stone could represent what the athletes were given when they won. This stone allowed them to enter the winner's celebration after the games. This brings to mind the marriage supper believers will participate in, the victorious celebration to the one who overcomes — **Revelation 19:7**.

Read **Revelation 2:12, Ephesians 6:17,** and **Hebrews 4:12.** To the church in Pergamum, why did Jesus identify Himself as "the one who has a sharp two-edged sword?"

_____
_____
_____
_____
_____
_____

Read **2 Timothy 3:16-17.** Why is the Word of God important?

_____
_____
_____
_____
_____
_____

Read **Revelation 2:14-16,** and **2 John 9-11.** God takes His Word very seriously. What warning does He give for people who go beyond the Word of God?

_____
_____
_____
_____
_____

. . . .

Read **John 14:15.** Why is tolerating sinful behavior a sin?

_____
_____
_____
_____
_____
_____

Read **Revelation 2:16.** What does "repent" mean?

_____
_____
_____
_____
_____
_____

Read **2 Corinthians 6:14-17.** What does God say about His people compromising with the world?

_____
_____
_____
_____
_____
_____

PRAYER: Father, thank You for sending Jesus to die on the cross for my sins. I repent of my sins and turn to You!

. . . .

FRIDAY: WITNESS

After WAKING UP, WORSHIPPING the Lord, and WAITING

upon the Lord it's time to WORK...

> "But you shall receive power when the Holy Spirit has come upon
> you; and you shall be WITNESSES to Me...to the end of the earth."
> **Acts 1:8 NKJV**

Read **Psalm 1:1.** Are you sensitive to sin? Explain and share a verse.

_____
_____
_____
_____
_____
_____

Read **Psalm 139:23-24.** Do you see your sin in the light of God's glory?
What sins are you tolerating in your life? Explain and share a verse.

_____
_____
_____
_____
_____
_____

Read **Matthew 18:15-17.** When you see your friends sinning against
God, do you tell them?

_____
_____
_____
_____
_____
_____

At school, do people try to sow seeds of doubt in your mind about
God? What should you do?

_____

. . . .

_____
_____
_____
_____
_____

Get together with your community group and decide how your group
is going to confront sin and not tolerate it.

_____
_____
_____
_____
_____
_____

With your community group discuss how you are going to handle
conversations with people who say: "What works for you is good and
what works for me is good." How will you declare truth to these
people? Share a verse.

_____
_____
_____
_____
_____
_____

Write your prayer:

_____
_____
_____
_____
_____
_____

. . . .

REVELATION
the End

. . . .

Week 7: Revelation 2:18-29

. . . .

MONDAY: WAKE UP

"WAKE UP, for the coming of our salvation is nearer now than when we first believed." **Romans 13:11 NLT**

Lord, please open my eyes to Your heart. Illuminate Your truths to me.

Speak Lord, Your servant listens.

Read: **Revelation 2:18-29**

What does the verse say?

_____
_____
_____
_____
_____
_____

What is the lesson?

_____
_____
_____
_____
_____
_____

What is God telling you?

_____
_____
_____
_____
_____
_____

. . . .

REVELATION
the End

What is your commitment?

_____
_____
_____
_____
_____
_____

. . . .

TUESDAY: WORSHIP

After WAKING UP, it's time to WORSHIP...

"But the hour is coming, and is now here, when the true worshippers will WORSHIP the Father in spirit and truth, for the Father is seeking such people to worship him." **John 4:23 ESV**

Near the Cross
Fanny Crosby, 1869

Jesus, keep me near the cross,
There a precious fountain,
Free to all, a healing stream,
Flows from Calvary's mountain.

Chorus:
In the cross, in the cross
Be my glory ever,
Till my ransomed soul shall find
Rest beyond the river.

Near the cross, a trembling soul,
Love and mercy found me;
There the Bright and Morning Star
Shed His beams around me.

Near the cross!
O Lamb of God,
Bring its scenes before me;
Help me walk from day to day
With its shadow o'er me.

Near the cross!
I'll watch and wait,
Hoping, trusting ever,
Till I reach the golden strand,
Just beyond the river.

....

Read **Revelation 2:28** and **Revelation 22:16.** Who is the Bright and Morning Star?

_____
_____
_____
_____
_____
_____

Why is it important for the believer to stay "near the cross"? Explain and share a verse.

_____
_____
_____
_____
_____
_____

Read **Galatians 6:14.** What should you boast of? Why?

_____
_____
_____
_____
_____
_____

If you were to write a couple lines to a worship song that included the gospel, what would you say?

_____
_____
_____
_____
_____
_____

PRAYER: Abba! Keep me near the cross, where love and mercy find me.

. . . .

WEDNESDAY: WAIT

After WAKING UP, WORSHIPPING, it's time to WAIT upon the Lord…

"But those who WAIT on the LORD shall renew their strength; they shall mount up with wings like eagles, they shall run and not be weary, they shall walk and not faint." **Isaiah 40:31 NKJV**

READ: **2 Peter 3:14**
Pray for your:

Family:

_____
_____
_____
_____
_____
_____

Friends:

_____
_____
_____
_____
_____
_____

Community Group:

_____
_____
_____
_____
_____
_____

…………

REVELATION
the End

Church:

_____
_____
_____
_____
_____
_____

Nation:

_____
_____
_____
_____
_____
_____

Leaders:

_____
_____
_____
_____
_____
_____

Yourself:

_____
_____
_____
_____
_____
_____

. . . .

THURSDAY: WORK

After WAKING UP, WORSHIPPING the Lord, and WAITING
upon the Lord, it's time to WORK...

"WORK hard so God can approve you. Be a good worker, one who
does not need to be ashamed and who correctly explains the word of
truth." **2 Timothy 2:15 NLT**

"Be Holy For I Am Holy!"
Read: **Revelation 2:18-29**

God's glory is seen in a pure church, a church that walks in holiness,
obeying Christ. A church like that is a light to the world — **Matthew
5:16**. In turn, God will remove IIis glory from a church immersed in
idolatry and immorality — **Ezekiel 10:18**. God commands His church,
"Be holy for I am holy" — **1 Peter 1:16**. So, this is serious. A sinful
church allowing false doctrine is subject to judgment — **Romans 6:23**.

Jesus takes His church's holiness seriously. He desires a pure bride —
Revelation 19:7. He sees everything that is going on in His church
and He moves quickly with feet of judgment to convict, correct, and
chasten the sin in its midst — **Revelation 1:15, 2:18**. So, He writes this
letter to the church in Thyatira, warning them of coming judgment if
they do not repent of their wicked ways — **Revelation 2:18, 21-22**.

He first commends them for their love, faith, service, and patient
endurance — **Revelation 2:19**. But then He brings His complaint, "You
are permitting that woman — that Jezebel who calls herself a
prophet — to lead my servants astray" — **Revelation 2:20a NLT**. This
leader in the church was encouraging the people to worship idols, eat
food offered to idols, and commit sexual sin — **Revelation 2:20**. And
the church was allowing it! They were permitting evil to take place in
their midst. Not good! The church is to uphold the truth. We are to
defend the truth, not compromise the truth.

In His grace, Jesus gave this leader time to repent and she refused —

....

Revelation 2:21. Christian, if God is speaking to you right now regarding the sin in your life, repent! Do not harden your heart to the voice of the Lord — **Hebrews 3:15**. For all have sinned and fallen short of the glory of God — **Romans 3:23 NKJV**. But in His love, He sent Jesus to die on the cross for you — **Romans 5:8**. God will judge unrepentant sinners — **Revelation 2:22, Romans 6:23**. Jesus forgives you when you repent! So, today, turn from your sin and turn to Christ — **Acts 17:30**!

To the minority in the church that dedicated themselves to holiness, Jesus calls out, "Keep the faith and you will rule and reign with Me" — **Revelation 2:24-28**. See, if you commit yourself to purity and holiness you will have genuine spiritual power to change lives. You will be able to speak with authority because you live a life of integrity and moral purity.

Christian, it's your job to examine yourself — **2 Corinthians 13:5**. Are you right with God? Search the Scriptures — **Acts 17:11**. Is your church teaching the truth? Take responsibility for your walk with God!

Read **Psalm 24:3-6.** Why does God demand holiness and purity in His church? What does this look like?

_____
_____
_____
_____
_____
_____

Read **Revelation 2:20** and **1 Kings 21:25-26.** In the Old Testament, Jezebel influenced the Jews to practice idolatry and immorality. What is this woman, who calls herself a prophetess, doing in the church of Thyatira? Why does God not like this? Explain and share a verse.

_____
_____
_____
_____
_____
_____

. . . .

When a church allows sin in its midst, how does this affect God's glory? Explain and share a verse.

_____
_____
_____
_____
_____
_____

Read **Matthew 18:15-17.** How should a holy church confront sin?

_____
_____
_____
_____
_____
_____

Read **Revelation 2:23** and **Jeremiah 17:10.** Explain these verses.

_____
_____
_____
_____
_____
_____

Read **Romans 2:5-11.** What does God tell His church?

_____
_____
_____
_____
_____
_____

To the minority of believers in Thyatira that did not listen to Jezebel's teaching but lived holy and pure lives — **Revelation 2:2**, Jesus says, "hold on to what you have until I come" (**Revelation 2:25**). How do you hold on to what you have?

_____
_____
_____

....

_____
_____
_____

Read **Hebrews 3:15** and **Revelation 2:29.** What do these verses mean? How are you to apply them to your life?

_____
_____
_____
_____
_____
_____

Prayer: Father, thank You for Your truth! Your Word gives me a strong foundation to identify what is false and what is right, in order to make wise decisions that will impact my life and others.

FRIDAY: WITNESS

After WAKING UP, WORSHIPPING the Lord, and WAITING

upon the Lord it's time to WORK...

"But you shall receive power when the Holy Spirit has come upon you; and you shall be **witnesses** to Me...to the end of the earth." **Acts 1:8 NKJV**

Read **Acts 17:11.** After listening to a message by a pastor or a teacher, do you go back to your bible to check to make sure what they said was biblically correct? Explain.

_____
_____
_____
_____
_____
_____

Are you struggling with idolatry or immorality? Repent and ask your community group to pray for you and to hold you accountable.

_____
_____
_____
_____
_____
_____

When you repent of sin, do you aggressively pursue holiness? What does this look like? Explain and share a verse.

_____
_____
_____
_____
_____
_____

Read **Ephesians 4:17-5:18.** How are we to walk in holiness as

....

Christians?

_____

_____

_____

_____

_____

_____

Can people identify you as a Christian? How? Explain.

_____

_____

_____

_____

_____

_____

How is your community group going to stand for Jesus Christ and truth at school? Do it and share what happened.

_____

_____

_____

_____

_____

_____

Read **John 15:19, Romans 12:1-2,** and **Titus 2:12.** How are you going to separate yourself from the world?

_____

_____

_____

_____

_____

_____

PRAYER: Father! Thank You for helping me stand up for the truth of Jesus Christ and separate myself from the world.

. . . .

Week 8: **Revelation 3:1-6**

. . . .

MONDAY: WAKE UP

"WAKE UP, for the coming of our salvation is nearer now than when we first believed." **Romans 13:11 NLT**

Lord, please open my eyes to Your heart. Illuminate Your truths to me. Speak Lord, Your servant listens.

Read: **Revelation 3:1-6**

What does the verse say?

_____
_____
_____
_____
_____
_____

What is the lesson?

_____
_____
_____
_____
_____
_____

What is God telling you?

_____
_____
_____
_____
_____
_____

. . . .

What is your commitment?

_____

_____

_____

_____

_____

_____

_____

. . . .

TUESDAY: WORSHIP

After WAKING UP, it's time to WORSHIP...

"But the hour is coming, and is now here, when the true worshippers will WORSHIP the Father in spirit and truth, for the Father is seeking such people to worship him." **John 4:23 ESV**

Faith is the Victory
John H. Yates, 1891

Encamped along the hills of light,
Ye Christian soldiers, rise
And press the battle ere the night
Shall veil the glowing skies.
Against the foe in vales below
Let all our strength be hurled;
Faith is the victory, we know,
That overcomes the world.

Chorus:
Faith is the victory! (Faith is the victory!)
Faith is the victory! (Faith is the victory!)
Oh, glorious victory
That overcomes the world.

His banner over us is love,
Our sword the Word of God;
We tread the road the saints above
With shouts of triumph trod.
By faith they, like a whirlwind's breath,
Swept on o'er every field;
The faith by which they conquered death
Is still our shining shield. [Chorus]

To him who overcomes the foe
White raiment shall be giv'n;

....

the End

Before the angels he shall know
His name confessed in heav'n
Then onward from the hills of light,
Our hearts with love aflame;
We'll vanquish all the hosts of night
In Jesus' conquering name. [Chorus]

Read **Revelation 3:4,** and **1 John 5:4-5**. How do Christians overcome
this evil world?

_____

_____

_____

_____

_____

_____

Read **Hebrews 11:1**. What is faith?

_____

_____

_____

_____

_____

Read **1 Peter 3:15**. Why does worshiping Jesus Christ as Lord of your
life give you a strong defense for your Christian hope?

_____

_____

_____

_____

_____

_____

PRAYER: Abba! Thank You for Your banner of love!

. . . .

WEDNESDAY: WAIT

After WAKING UP, WORSHIPPING, it's time to WAIT upon the Lord…

"But those who WAIT on the LORD shall renew their strength; they shall mount up with wings like eagles, they shall run and not be weary, they shall walk and not faint." **Isaiah 40:31 NKJV**

READ: **2 Chronicles 7:14**
Pray for your:

Family:

_____
_____
_____
_____
_____
_____

Friends:

_____
_____
_____
_____
_____
_____

Community Group:

_____
_____
_____
_____
_____
_____

. . . .

REVELATION
the End

Church:

_____
_____
_____
_____
_____
_____

Nation:

_____
_____
_____
_____
_____
_____

Leaders:

_____
_____
_____
_____
_____
_____

Yourself:

_____
_____
_____
_____
_____
_____

. . . .

THURSDAY: WORK

After WAKING UP, WORSHIPPING the Lord, and WAITING upon the Lord, it's time to WORK...

"WORK hard so God can approve you. Be a good worker, one who does not need to be ashamed and who correctly explains the word of truth." **2 Timothy 2:15 NLT**

Awaken!
Read: **Revelation 3:1-6**

Jesus called the church in Sardis a dead church. Can you believe that?! The people were going to church, but were considered dead spiritually! Their church was not witnessing the glory of God.

Is your church experiencing the glory of God? Are you? Or do you need a revival? Christian, it only takes one heart on fire to start a revival! As Lawrence Tribble wrote in the late 1700's:

One man awake, awakens another.
The second awakens his next door brother.
The three awake can rouse a town,
By turning the whole place upside down.
The many awake can cause such a fuss,
It finally awakens the rest of us.
One man up, with dawn in his eyes,
Surely then
Multiplies.

God said, "Then if my people who are called by my name will humble themselves and pray and seek my face and turn from their wicked ways, I will hear from heaven and will forgive their sins and heal their land"—**2 Chronicles 7:14 NLT**.

It simply takes one person hearing the voice of the Lord and acting on

....

it. Christian, be of good cheer! God can bring dead things back to life!

Read **Revelation 3:2-3.** Jesus is calling the church of Sardis to wake up and remember the foundation of their faith:

Read **Matthew 1:23, John 1:14, John 10:30** (See also: **2 Corinthians 5:21, Ephesians 1:20-21, John 14:1-4**). What is the truth about Jesus?

_____

_____

_____

_____

_____

_____

Read **Romans 5:6-9.** What is salvation?

_____

_____

_____

_____

_____

_____

Read **Romans 3:23.** What is sin?

_____

_____

_____

_____

_____

_____

Read **Romans 5:1** (See also: **Acts 13:38-39** and **Hebrews 10:17**). What is justification?

_____

_____

_____

_____

_____

_____

. . . .

Read **2 Thessalonians 2:13.** What is sanctification?

_____
_____
_____
_____
_____
_____

Read **Revelation 3:3.** What happens if a person does not repent of their sin and turn back to God?

_____
_____
_____
_____
_____
_____

Read **Revelation 3:5,** and **Mark 9:3.** What do the white garments represent?

_____
_____
_____
_____
_____
_____

Read **Revelation 3:5,** and **Luke 10:20** (See also: **Psalm 139:16,** and **Daniel 12:1**). What is the Book of Life?

_____
_____
_____
_____
_____
_____

Prayer: Thank You Lord for hearing my prayers!

....

FRIDAY: WITNESS

After WAKING UP, WORSHIPPING the Lord, and WAITING

upon the Lord it's time to WORK...

> "But you shall receive power when the Holy Spirit has come upon
> you; and you shall be WINESSES to Me...to the end of the earth."
> **Acts 1:8 NKJV**

When did you accept Jesus Christ into your life? Share your
testimony.

_____

_____

_____

_____

_____

_____

Read **Revelation 3:1, Matthew 18:15-17,** and **James 5:16.** It is
dangerous when a church has lost interest in its personal holiness.
Unrepentant sin kills a good life. What is God calling His church to
do? What is He calling you to do?

_____

_____

_____

_____

_____

_____

Read **1 John 1:8-9.** Do you look good on the outside, but you know
your heart isn't right with the Lord? What do you need to do?

_____

_____

_____

_____

_____

_____

. . . .

Read **2 Chronicles 7:14.** How does a "dead church" or a "spiritually dead person" come alive?

_____
_____
_____
_____
_____
_____

Are you struggling in your walk? Call a Christian friend who is on fire with the Lord and ask them to share what they are learning in the Word. When one heart is on fire it ignites another!

Read **Matthew 5:13-16.** What does a genuine Christian look like?

_____
_____
_____
_____
_____
_____

Read **Galatians 5:22-23.** How do you know the Holy Spirit is alive and moving through a church, community, or a person?

_____
_____
_____
_____
_____
_____

Read **Revelation 3:4-5, Malachi 3:16-17,** and **Hebrews 6:10.** God does not forget those who remain faithful to Him. Share this truth with a family member or friend.

Prayer: Thank You Lord for forgiving me of my sins! I choose to surrender my life to You for Your glory!

....

REVELATION
the End

Week 9: **Revelation 3:7-13**

. . . .

MONDAY: WAKE UP

"WAKE UP, for the coming of our salvation is nearer now than when we first believed." **Romans 13:11 NLT**

Lord, please open my eyes to Your heart. Illuminate Your truths to me.
Speak Lord, Your servant listens.

Read: **Revelation 3:7-13**

What does the verse say?

_____
_____
_____
_____
_____
_____

What is the lesson?

_____
_____
_____
_____
_____
_____

What is God telling you?

_____
_____
_____
_____
_____
_____

. . . .

What is your commitment?

_____

_____

_____

_____

_____

_____

_____

. . . .

TUESDAY: WORSHIP

After WAKING UP, it's time to WORSHIP…

"But the hour is coming, and is now here, when the true worshippers will WORSHIP the Father in spirit and truth, for the Father is seeking such people to worship him." **John 4:23 ESV**

I Need Thee Every Hour
Annie S. Hawks, 1872

I need Thee every hour,
Most gracious Lord;
No tender voice like Thine
Can peace afford.

Chorus:
I need Thee, O I need Thee;
Ev'ry hour I need Thee!
O bless me now, my Savior,
I come to Thee.

I need Thee ev'ry hour,
Stay Thou nearby;
Temptations lose their pow'r
When Thou art nigh.

[Chorus]

I need Thee ev'ry hour,
In joy or pain;
Come quickly and abide,
Or life is vain.

[Chorus]

I need Thee ev'ry hour,

…………

Teach me Thy will;
Thy promises so rich
In me fulfill.

[Chorus]

I need Thee ev'ry hour,
Most Holy One;
O make me Thine indeed,
Thou blessed Son.

Why do we need Jesus "ev'ry hour"?

_____
_____
_____
_____
_____
_____

Read **Hebrews 4:16.** What should we do as children of God?

_____
_____
_____
_____
_____
_____

Read **Revelation 3:10.** What does Jesus promise to do?

_____
_____
_____
_____
_____
_____

PRAYER: Abba! Please bend down and hear my prayer, answering me,

for I need Your help!

. . . .

WEDNESDAY: WAIT

After WAKING UP, WORSHIPPING, it's time to WAIT upon the Lord…

"But those who WAIT on the LORD shall renew their strength; they shall mount up with wings like eagles, they shall run and not be weary, they shall walk and not faint." **Isaiah 40:31 NKJV**

READ: **Matthew 7:7-8**
Pray for your:

Family:

_____
_____
_____
_____
_____
_____

Friends:

_____
_____
_____
_____
_____
_____

Community Group:

_____
_____
_____
_____
_____
_____

…………

REVELATION
the End

Church:

_____
_____
_____
_____
_____
_____
_____

Nation:

_____
_____
_____
_____
_____
_____
_____

Leaders:

_____
_____
_____
_____
_____
_____
_____

Yourself:

_____
_____
_____
_____
_____
_____
_____

. . . .

THURSDAY: WORK

After WAKING UP, WORSHIPPING the Lord, and WAITING

upon the Lord, it's time to WORK...

"WORK hard so God can approve you. Be a good worker, one who does not need to be ashamed and who correctly explains the word of truth." **2 Timothy 2:15 NLT**

The Church in Philadelphia
Read: **Revelation 3:7-13**

If you were asked to share a short devotional on the church in Philadelphia, what would you say? Look at your notes from Monday to help in writing your devotional. Share with your community group.

_____

_____

_____

_____

_____

_____

_____

_____

_____

_____

_____

_____

_____

_____

_____

_____

_____

_____

_____

_____

_____

_____

_____

_____

....

REVELATION

the End

....

_____

_____

Read **Revelation 3:7-8, Matthew 7:7-8, 1 John 5:14-15** (See also **Luke 18:1, Psalm 34:15, 17, John 16:23-24**) How are "doors" opened?

_____

_____

_____

_____

_____

_____

Revelation 3:8 NLT "You obeyed my word." Why is obedience to the Word of God so important? Explain and share a verse.

_____

_____

_____

_____

_____

_____

Read **Revelation 3:10.** In this verse, Jesus promises that His church will not have to face the Tribulation, but will be delivered from it. What does the Bible say about the Rapture of the church? Read **John 14:1-4, 1 Corinthians 15:51-54, 1 Thessalonians 4:13-17.**

_____

_____

_____

_____

_____

_____

PRAYER: Thank You Lord for opening doors no man can shut and shutting doors no man can open. Thank you for my salvation! I am eternally secure in Your hands.

....

REVELATION

the End

FRIDAY: WITNESS

After WAKING UP, WORSHIPPING the Lord, WAITING upon
the Lord, and WORKING, it's time to WITNESS!

> "But you shall receive power when the Holy Spirit has come upon
> you; and you shall be WITNESSES to Me...to the end of the earth."
> **Acts 1:8 NKJV**

Read **1 Peter 1:15. Revelation 3:7** describes Jesus as "He who is holy."
Because Jesus is holy, His church must be holy. How are you going to
walk in holiness? Share a verse.

_____

_____

_____

_____

_____

_____

Read **Revelation 3:7.** What "doors" have God shut in your life? In
looking back, do you see His wisdom in doing so? Share.

_____

_____

_____

_____

_____

_____

Read **Revelation 3:8.** What "doors" have God opened for you? Share
your story.

_____

_____

_____

_____

_____

_____

. . . .

Read **2 Corinthians 12:8-10. Revelation 3:8 NLT** "You have little strength." Share a time when God's power worked through your weaknesses.

_____
_____
_____
_____
_____
_____

Revelation 3:8 NLT "You obeyed my word and did not deny me." What is God calling you to obey Him in right now? Share.

_____
_____
_____
_____
_____
_____

Read **Matthew 10:22,** and **Hebrews 12:1-4. Revelation 3:10 NIV** says, "you have kept my command to endure patiently." Are you patiently enduring trials? How is Jesus an example for us in patient endurance? How will you "endure to the end?"

_____
_____
_____
_____
_____
_____

Read **Colossians 4:2-3** and pray for doors to be opened for your community group to share the gospel with the lost.

_____
_____
_____
_____
_____
_____

....

REVELATION
the End

Week 10: Revelation 3:14-22

. . . .

MONDAY: WAKE UP

"WAKE UP, for the coming of our salvation is nearer now than when we first believed." **Romans 13:11 NLT**

Lord, please open my eyes to Your heart. Illuminate Your truths to me.

Speak Lord, Your servant listens.

Read: **Revelation 3:14-22**

What does the verse say?

_____

_____

_____

_____

_____

_____

What is the lesson?

_____

_____

_____

_____

_____

_____

What is God telling you?

_____

_____

_____

_____

_____

. . . .

REVELATION
the End

What is your commitment?

....

TUESDAY: WORSHIP

After WAKING UP, it's time to WORSHIP...

"But the hour is coming, and is now here, when the true worshippers will WORSHIP the Father in spirit and truth, for the Father is seeking such people to worship him." **John 4:23 ESV**

Open Wide the Door
Barney E. Warren, 1897

Sinner, hark! The Savior's calling,
Pleading o'er and o'er;
Hear those tender accents falling:
"Open wide the door."

Refrain:
Humbly bow with broken spirit,
Heaven's mercy to implore;
Jesus calls, O sinner, hear it!
Open wide the door.

Weary sinner, lost and sighing,
Hear the call *once* more;
See the Savior bleeding, dying;
Open wide the door.

Wake, the joy fore'er increasing,
On the blissful shore;
Give thyself in Jesus' keeping;
Open wide the door.
Hear the gospel message given,
Bar it out no more;
Christ will speak thy sins forgiven;
Open wide the door.

. . . .

Read **Revelation 3:15-16**. Have you ever experienced a "lukewarm" season in your walk? How did that impact your worship?

_____
_____
_____
_____
_____
_____

Read **Revelation 3:20.** What does this verse mean?

_____
_____
_____
_____
_____
_____

Explain a time when you heard the Lord calling out to you to worship Him?

_____
_____
_____
_____
_____
_____

Explain why we worship God with song. What other ways can we worship Him?

_____
_____
_____
_____
_____
_____

PRAYER: Lord! Thank You for wanting to spend time with me.

WEDNESDAY: WAIT

After WAKING UP, WORSHIPPING, it's time to WAIT upon the Lord…

"But those who WAIT on the LORD shall renew their strength; they shall mount up with wings like eagles, they shall run and not be weary, they shall walk and not faint." **Isaiah 40:31 NKJV**

READ: **Ephesians 5:14-20**
Pray for your:

Family:

_____
_____
_____
_____
_____
_____

Friends:

_____
_____
_____
_____
_____
_____

Community Group:

_____
_____
_____
_____
_____
_____

....

REVELATION
the End

Church:

_____
_____
_____
_____
_____
_____
_____

Nation:

_____
_____
_____
_____
_____
_____
_____

Leaders:

_____
_____
_____
_____
_____
_____
_____

Yourself:

_____
_____
_____
_____
_____
_____
_____

. . . .

THURSDAY: WORK

After WAKING UP, WORSHIPPING the Lord, and WAITING

upon the Lord, it's time to WORK...

"WORK hard so God can approve you. Be a good worker, one who does not need to be ashamed and who correctly explains the word of truth." **2 Timothy 2:15 NLT**

The Church in Laodicea
Read: **Revelation 3:14-22**

If you were asked to share a short devotional on the church in Laodicea, what would you say? Look at your notes from Sunday's message and at your notes from Monday to help in writing your devotional. Share with your community group.

_____
_____
_____
_____
_____
_____
_____
_____
_____
_____
_____
_____
_____
_____
_____
_____
_____
_____
_____
_____
_____
_____

. . . .

REVELATION
the End

Read **Revelation 3:15-17, James 2:14** and **Matthew 7:16-20.** What does the Bible say about identifying a person's true spiritual state?

_____

_____

_____

_____

_____

_____

In **Revelation 3:17**, Jesus tells the church of Laodicea that they are "wretched, miserable, poor, blind, and naked." What does He tell them to do in **Revelation 3:18**? Why?

_____

_____

_____

_____

_____

_____

Read **Revelation 3:20.** Jesus is knocking on the door of the church of Laodicea, asking to come in. He's waiting for the church to repent. Jesus is pursuing this church. Where else in Scripture do we find the Lord pursuing sinners in love? Share.

_____

_____

_____

_____

_____

_____

PRAYER: Thank you Lord for pursuing me and calling me to repentance.

. . . .

FRIDAY: WITNESS

After WAKING UP, WORSHIPPING the Lord, WAITING upon the Lord, and WORKING, it's time to WITNESS!

"But you shall receive power when the Holy Spirit has come upon you; and you shall be WITNESSES to Me...to the end of the earth."
Acts 1:8 NKJV

Read **Revelation 3:15-16.** How would you rate your "spiritual temperature"? Are you hot, cold, or lukewarm?

_____
_____
_____
_____
_____
_____

What does a person, whose spiritual temperature is "hot," look like? Share a verse.

_____
_____
_____
_____
_____
_____

What does a person, whose spiritual temperature is "cold," look like? Share a verse.

_____
_____
_____
_____
_____
_____

What does a person, whose spiritual temperature is "lukewarm," look

. . . .

like? Share a verse.

_____

_____

_____

_____

_____

_____

If everyone in your church or your community group had your same spiritual temperature, what would it look like? Would a revival break out? Would people be getting saved? Would people be welcomed? Would people be prayed for and ministered to? Or would the people just come to church and leave, never talking to anyone about Jesus?

_____

_____

_____

_____

_____

_____

Do you take Jesus Christ seriously? The cross seriously? The Bible? Sin? Share a verse.

_____

_____

_____

_____

_____

_____

Revelation 3:19 says "Be zealous and repent." Pray for your community group to "be zealous" for Christ, repenting of sin.

_____

_____

_____

_____

_____

_____

....

REVELATION
the End

. . . .

Week 11: Revelation 4:1-11

. . . .

MONDAY: WAKE UP

"WAKE UP, for the coming of our salvation is nearer now than when we first believed." **Romans 13:11 NLT**

Lord, please open my eyes to Your heart. Illuminate Your truths to me.
Speak Lord, Your servant listens.

Read: **Revelation 4:1-11**

What does the verse say?

_____
_____
_____
_____
_____
_____

What is the lesson?

_____
_____
_____
_____
_____
_____

What is God telling you?

_____
_____
_____
_____
_____
_____

. . . .

What is your commitment?

_____
_____
_____
_____
_____
_____
_____

. . . .

TUESDAY: WORSHIP

After WAKING UP, it's time to WORSHIP...

"But the hour is coming, and is now here, when the true worshippers will WORSHIP the Father in spirit and truth, for the Father is seeking such people to worship him." **John 4:23 ESV**

Holy, Holy, Holy!
Reginald Heber, 1826

Holy, holy, holy! Lord God Almighty!
Early in the morning our song shall rise to Thee;
Holy, holy, holy! Merciful and mighty!
God in three persons, blessed Trinity!

Holy, holy, holy! All the saints adore Thee,
Casting down their golden crowns around the glassy sea;
Cherubim and seraphim falling down before Thee,
Which wert and art and evermore shalt be.

Holy, holy, holy! Though the darkness hide Thee,
Though the eye of sinful man Thy glory may not see:
Only Thou art holy; there is none beside Thee,
Perfect in pow'r, in love, and purity.

Holy, holy, holy! Lord God Almighty!
All Thy works shall praise Thy name in earth and sky and sea.
Holy, holy, holy! Merciful and mighty!
God in three persons, blessed Trinity!

Read **Revelation 4**. What does being in God's presence look like?

_____

_____

_____

_____

....

Read **Isaiah 6:1-8.** How does Isaiah describe being in God's presence?

_____

_____

_____

_____

_____

_____

Read **1 Samuel 2:2.** Is there anyone "holy like the LORD"? Explain.

_____

_____

_____

_____

_____

_____

Read **Psalm 103:22** and **Psalm 145:10.** Today, how are you going to worship and praise the Lord?

_____

_____

_____

_____

_____

_____

Write your prayer:

_____

_____

_____

_____

_____

_____

. . . .

WEDNESDAY: WAIT

After WAKING UP, WORSHIPPING, it's time to WAIT upon the Lord…

> "But those who WAIT on the LORD shall renew their strength; they shall mount up with wings like eagles, they shall run and not be weary, they shall walk and not faint." **Isaiah 40:31 NKJV**

READ: **Colossians 1:15-18**
Pray for your:

Family:

_____
_____
_____
_____
_____
_____

Friends:

_____
_____
_____
_____
_____
_____

Community Group:

_____
_____
_____
_____
_____
_____

…………

REVELATION
the End

Church:

_____
_____
_____
_____
_____
_____

Nation:

_____
_____
_____
_____
_____
_____

Leaders:

_____
_____
_____
_____
_____
_____

Yourself:

_____
_____
_____
_____
_____
_____

. . . .

THURSDAY: WORK

After WAKING UP, WORSHIPPING the Lord, and WAITING upon the Lord, it's time to WORK...

"WORK hard so God can approve you. Be a good worker, one who does not need to be ashamed and who correctly explains the word of truth." **2 Timothy 2:15 NLT**

God's Presence Ignites Passion!
Read: **Revelation 4**

We are here on earth to know God, and to make Him known. Our purpose in life is found in our relationship with Him. It's His presence that we long for; it's heaven on earth. We want people to experience this joy — **Psalm 16:11**. So, we are vessels, ready for the Lord to use, housing the treasure of the gospel, reaching out to the lost — **2 Timothy 2:21, Matthew 28:19**. God's presence has ignited a passion in our hearts; our message is urgent, and we cannot be silenced. We are soldiers for Christ on mission: to wake up those that are sleeping, for heaven is near — **Ephesians 5:14**.

Heaven is God's presence and Jesus is the key that unlocks the door — **Revelation 4:1, John 14:6**. In **Revelation 4**, John hears God's voice and is instantly in heaven in the throne room of God. John sees God sitting on the throne in complete control over everything. He is overwhelmed by God's glory and majesty — **Revelation 4:3**. Twenty-four thrones surround God, and here John sees the fulfillment of God's promise to protect His people from the time of the Tribulation — **Revelation 4:4, Revelation 3:10**. John beholds the redeemed, the Christians who are raptured to heaven.

Clothed in white and wearing gold crowns — **Revelation 4:4**, John sees the redeemed as God sees them, holy and pure — **Ephesians 1:4**; washed by the blood of Jesus Christ — **Isaiah 1:18**. They are perfect. Free from judgment. No more tears — **Revelation 21:4**. They boldly

....

stand in God's presence, passionate about their King — **Hebrews 4:16, Revelation 4:10-11**.

Then in front of the throne John observes flashes of lightning and thunder. He identifies seven lampstands with burning flames and the seven spirits of God — **Revelation 4:5-6**. It's here that John witnesses the storm of God's fury that is to come upon the earth; God's divine wrath and judgment that is about to war with rebellious sinful mankind, who have rejected Him.

John's attention is turned to the four living beings that are around the throne — **Revelation 4:6-8**. He watches these majestic beings honor and worship God day and night, saying "Holy, holy, holy, Lord God Almighty, who was and is and is to come" — **Revelation 4:8 NKJV**! Worshiping God is their primary responsibility, their calling. It's what they are made to do. And as these four cherubim work in their calling, giving glory and honor and thanks to God — **Revelation 4:9**, the redeemed fall down in reverence, casting their crowns at God's feet saying, "You are worthy, O Lord our God" — **Revelation 4:11 NLT**. As John witnesses the attitude of humility and adoration at the foot of God's throne, he sees the passion that comes from being in God's presence. This is heaven.

We Christians long for heaven. But we have work to do right now. The world cannot stop passionate Christians that are zealous for the Lord and His glory. So we are soldiers for Christ on mission: to wake up those that are sleeping, with the message of the gospel, for heaven is near — **Ephesians 5:14**.

What is the gospel message? Include verses.

_____
_____
_____
_____
_____
_____

. . . .

Read **Ezekiel 1.** Ezekiel describes his vision of the throne room of God in great detail. Compare Ezekiel's vision to John's vision in **Revelation 4.** After being in the presence of God, what do they both talk about? Why is this important?

_____
_____
_____
_____
_____
_____

Read **Revelation 4:1** and **John 10:9.** Who opens the door to heaven? Explain.

_____
_____
_____
_____
_____
_____

In **Revelation 4:10,** the 24 elders cast their crowns at God's feet. Describe the crowns we will be casting at God's feet? Read:

1 Corinthians 9:24-27 - the Incorruptible Crown:

_____
_____
_____
_____
_____
_____

Philippians 4:1, and **1 Thessalonians 2:19 -** the Crown of Rejoicing:

_____
_____
_____
_____
_____
_____

. . . .

2 Timothy 4:8 - the Crown of Righteousness:

_____
_____
_____
_____
_____
_____

James 1:12 and Revelation 2:10- the Crown of Life:

_____
_____
_____
_____
_____

1 Peter 5:1-4- the Crown of Glory:

_____
_____
_____
_____
_____

Prayer: Open the eyes of my heart Lord, I want to see You!

. . . .

FRIDAY: WITNESS

After WAKING UP, WORSHIPPING the Lord, WAITING upon the Lord, and WORKING, it's time to WITNESS!

> "But you shall receive power when the Holy Spirit has come upon you; and you shall be WITNESSES to Me...to the end of the earth."
> **Acts 1:8 NKJV**

Only the Christian has complete assurance that they will spend eternity in the presence of God. Do you have this assurance? Share.

_____
_____
_____
_____
_____
_____

How is your community group going to be soldiers for Christ on mission: waking up those that are sleeping with the message of the gospel?

_____
_____
_____
_____
_____
_____

Read **Psalm 46:10.** John heard God's voice in **Revelation 4:1**, and it drew him into God's presence. God is always speaking. What is He telling you today?

_____
_____
_____
_____
_____
_____

....

When you sit in God's presence, are there certain things that distract you from hearing His voice? Share.

_____
_____
_____
_____
_____
_____

The word throne, which symbolizes God's sovereignty and authority over everything, is mentioned 12 times in **Revelation 4.** Are you submitting to God's authority over your life? Or are you rebelling?

_____
_____
_____
_____
_____
_____

Read **Genesis 9:11-17.** The word rainbow in **Revelation 4:3** is a symbol of God's promise. God always keeps His promises. Which one of God's promises are you holding on to today?

_____
_____
_____
_____
_____
_____

Read **Revelation 4:10.** Today, how will you practically walk in humility, casting your crown at God's feet – recognizing that all of the rewards, recognition, accomplishments and success you achieve in life really belong to Him—**James 1:17**?

_____
_____
_____
_____
_____

. . . .

How are you preparing for heaven? Share a verse.

_____
_____
_____
_____
_____
_____

Prayer: Father! Every reward and recognition I have received, I give back to You, for You are the One who is Worthy.

. . . .

REVELATION
the End

....

Week 12: **Revelation 5**

. . . .

MONDAY: WAKE UP

"WAKE UP, for the coming of our salvation is nearer now than when we first believed." **Romans 13:11 NLT**

Lord, please open my eyes to Your heart. Illuminate Your truths to me.

Speak Lord, Your servant listens.

Read: **Revelation 5**

What does the verse say?

_____
_____
_____
_____
_____
_____

What is the lesson?

_____
_____
_____
_____
_____
_____

What is God telling you?

_____
_____
_____
_____
_____
_____

. . . .

What is your commitment?

_____

_____

_____

_____

_____

_____

. . . .

TUESDAY: WORSHIP

After WAKING UP, it's time to WORSHIP...

"But the hour is coming, and is now here, when the true worshippers will WORSHIP the Father in spirit and truth, for the Father is seeking such people to worship him." **John 4:23 ESV**

Love Divine, All Loves Excelling
Charles Wesley, 1747

Love divine, all loves excelling,
Joy of heaven, to earth come down;
Fix in us Thy humble dwelling;
All Thy faithful mercies crown.
Jesus, Thou art all compassion,
Pure, unbounded love Thou art;
Visit us with Thy salvation;
Enter every trembling heart.

Breathe, O breathe Thy loving Spirit
Into every troubled breast!
Let us all in Thee inherit,
Let us find the promised rest.
Take away our bent to sinning;
Alpha and Omega be;
End of faith, as its beginning,
Set our hearts at liberty.

Come, Almighty to deliver,
Let us all Thy grace receive;
Suddenly return, and never,
Nevermore thy temples leave.
Thee we would be always blessing,
Serve Thee as Thy hosts above,
Pray, and praise Thee without ceasing,
Glory in Thy perfect love.

. . . .

Finish, then, Thy new creation;
Pure and spotless let us be;
Let us see Thy great salvation
Perfectly restored in Thee:
Changed from glory into glory,
Till in heaven we take our place,
Till we cast our crowns before Thee,
Lost in wonder love and praise.

What is your favorite phrase in this hymn? Why?

_____

_____

_____

_____

_____

_____

The Psalms teach us how to worship and pray to God. Read **Psalm 103.** What does this passage reveal to you about God?

_____

_____

_____

_____

_____

_____

After reading this passage, what changes do you need to make in your acts of worship? (Is your worship genuine and sincere, focused on Jesus? Or are you focused on the people around you?)

_____

_____

_____

_____

_____

_____

PRAYER: Abba, help me to focus on You and only You during worship!

. . . .

WEDNESDAY: WAIT

After WAKING UP, WORSHIPPING, it's time to WAIT upon the Lord…

"But those who WAIT on the LORD shall renew their strength; they shall mount up with wings like eagles, they shall run and not be weary, they shall walk and not faint." **Isaiah 40:31 NKJV**

READ: **Jeremiah 33:3**
Pray for your:

Family:

_____
_____
_____
_____
_____
_____

Friends:

_____
_____
_____
_____
_____
_____

Community Group:

_____
_____
_____
_____
_____
_____

…………

REVELATION
the End

Church:

_____
_____
_____
_____
_____
_____
_____

Nation:

_____
_____
_____
_____
_____
_____
_____

Leaders:

_____
_____
_____
_____
_____
_____
_____

Yourself:

_____
_____
_____
_____
_____
_____
_____

. . . .

THURSDAY: WORK

After WAKING UP, WORSHIPPING the Lord, and WAITING upon the Lord, it's time to WORK...

"WORK hard so God can approve you. Be a good worker, one who does not need to be ashamed and who correctly explains the word of truth." **2 Timothy 2:15 NLT**

Look to Jesus!
Read: **Revelation 5**

In heaven, John sees God sitting on His throne, holding a scroll in His right hand. John's attention is drawn to the scroll, which is sealed with seven seals preventing unauthorized viewing. This scroll could very well be the title deed to the earth. Then a strong angel shouts out, "Who is worthy to open the scroll?" And John freaks out; he starts to cry because no one could be found in heaven and on earth worthy enough to open the scroll. He is weeping profusely because he cannot see the answer to the problem—**Revelation 5:1-4**. Have you ever gotten upset because you did not see the answer to the problem you were facing? You were so confused by the circumstances surrounding you that you wanted to throw in the towel and give up?

In heaven, one of the 24 elders walks up to John and says, "Stop crying! Look, the Lion of the tribe of Judah, the heir to David's throne, has conquered. The Messiah is here, Jesus Christ. He is worthy to open the scroll and break its seven seals"—**Revelation 5:5**. John looked, and he saw the Lamb that had been slain—**Revelation 5:6**. He saw Jesus. Jesus is alive! Are you looking for Jesus? Christian, don't let your emotions control you. Don't lean on your own understanding—**Proverbs 3:5-6**. Purposefully look to Jesus. Jesus is the answer to every problem.

Jesus steps forward, still bearing the marks of the crucifixion, and He takes the scroll. He is the One who is worthy because He shed His blood for sinful mankind; He has the authority to break the seals on the scroll that will release judgment on the earth. So here is Jesus walking around heaven in authority and majesty, and the four-living beings and the redeemed fall down before Him singing a new song, a song of redemption — **Revelation 5:7-9**.

John is surrounded by worship and adoration of the Lord. The humility, reverence, and awe of the four living beings and the redeemed all point to the glory and majesty of God and the sacrificial love of the Lamb, Jesus Christ. The worship is breathtaking — **Revelation 5:9-14**.

Christian, has God been less to you than what He has promised? Has He not heard and answered your prayers? Are you not promised heaven? Then worship Him today! Worship stops the downward spiral self-focus brings; it gets your eyes off of yourself and your problems, placing them on the One who is Worthy. As you worship, your eyes focus on Jesus and the nature of God. You are reminded of the greatness of God and you get the right perspective. Jesus is the answer. Look to Jesus.

Read **Revelation 5:6, Isaiah 53:7,** and **John 1:29.** Who is the Lamb?

_____
_____
_____
_____
_____
_____

Read **Revelation 5:6** Jesus is alive! What is salvation and why do Christians have the hope of heaven? Include verses.

_____
_____
_____
_____
_____
_____

. . . .

Read **Revelation 5:9, Matthew 28:18,** and **Philippians 2:9-11.** The scroll could very well be the title deed to the earth. Who alone has the authority to break the seals and open the scroll? Why?

_____

_____

_____

_____

_____

_____

Read **Revelation 5:8, Daniel 10:12** and **Psalm 27:8.** The Bible assures us that God hears our prayers. If God is all knowing, and all-powerful, why does He ask us to pray? Share a verse.

_____

_____

_____

_____

_____

_____

Read **Revelation 5:8-14** and **John 4:23.** What does it mean to worship God in spirit and in truth?

_____

_____

_____

_____

_____

_____

Revelation 4:11 says that God is "worthy" to "receive glory and honor and power." And **Revelation 5:12** says "The Lamb is worthy...to receive power and riches and wisdom and strength and honor and glory and blessing." Share why both God and Jesus are the only One worthy of such praise and worship. Include verses.

_____

_____

_____

_____

_____

. . . .

Read **Revelation 5:13** and **Philippians 2:9-11.** What does God promise in these verses?

_____

_____

_____

_____

_____

_____

Prayer: Jesus, in the midst of my problems I look to You, for You alone are worthy!

FRIDAY: WITNESS

After WAKING UP, WORSHIPPING the Lord, and WAITING

upon the Lord it's time to WORK...

> "But you shall receive power when the Holy Spirit has come upon
> you; and you shall be WITNESSES to Me...to the end of the earth."
> **Acts 1:8 NKJV**

After reading **Revelation 4** and **5,** how are you going to explain
heaven and God's presence to your family member or friend?

_____
_____
_____
_____
_____
_____

In **Revelation 5:4** John was upset. How are you going to encourage
your family member or friend who is struggling in a trial? What
verses will you share with them?

_____
_____
_____
_____
_____
_____

The sincerity of your times of worship and prayer reveal your true
devotion. Are you devoted to Jesus? Share.

_____
_____
_____
_____
_____
_____

....

the End

What is your favorite worship song? Why?

_____
_____
_____
_____
_____
_____

Read **Daniel 10:12-14.** Why does God call us to continue to pray and not give up? What are you continuing to pray for?

_____
_____
_____
_____
_____
_____

God makes everything beautiful in His timing — **Ecclesiastes 3:11.** How has God recently answered one of your prayers? Share a verse.

_____
_____
_____
_____
_____
_____

Read **Revelation 5:9, Psalm 33:3,** and **Psalm 96:1.** When God redeems us and delivers us from trials, we praise Him! We sing to Him a "new song." Has God recently delivered you from a trial? How are you going to praise Him?

_____
_____
_____
_____
_____
_____

PRAYER: Thank You King, for the privilege of worship and prayer!

. . . .

Week 13: **Revelation 6**

. . . .

MONDAY: WAKE UP

"WAKE UP, for the coming of our salvation is nearer now than when we first believed." **Romans 13:11 NLT**

Lord, please open my eyes to Your heart. Illuminate Your truths to me.

Speak Lord, Your servant listens.

Read: **Revelation 6**

What does the verse say?

_____

_____

_____

_____

_____

_____

What is the lesson?

_____

_____

_____

_____

_____

_____

What is God telling you?

_____

_____

_____

_____

_____

_____

. . . .

What is your commitment?

_____
_____
_____
_____
_____
_____

. . . .

TUESDAY: WORSHIP

After WAKING UP, it's time to WORSHIP...

"But the hour is coming, and is now here, when the true worshippers will WORSHIP the Father in spirit and truth, for the Father is seeking such people to worship him." **John 4:23 ESV**

I'd Rather Have Jesus
Rhea F. Miller, 1922

I'd rather have Jesus than silver or gold;
I'd rather be His than have riches untold;
I'd rather have Jesus than houses or lands;
I'd rather be led by His nail-pierced hand

Refrain:
Than to be the king of a vast domain
And be held in sin's dread sway;
I'd rather have Jesus than anything
This world affords today.

I'd rather have Jesus than men's applause;
I'd rather be faithful to His dear cause;
I'd rather have Jesus than worldwide fame;
I'd rather be true to His holy name

He's fairer than lilies of rarest bloom;
He's sweeter than honey from out of the comb;
He's all that my hungering spirit needs;
I'd rather have Jesus and let Him lead

Read **Revelation 6.** Judgment is coming to those who live for this world and not for Jesus. Friends don't let friends die without Jesus. Share the gospel with a friend today.

....

REVELATION
the End

_____
_____
_____
_____
_____
_____

Read **Matthew 16:25-26.** How will you apply these verses to your life?

_____
_____
_____
_____
_____

Read **Philippians 3:8.** Explain this verse.

_____
_____
_____
_____
_____

Can you truly say, "I'd rather have Jesus than silver or gold"? Share.

_____
_____
_____
_____
_____

Write your prayer:

_____
_____
_____
_____
_____

. . . .

WEDNESDAY: WAIT

After WAKING UP, WORSHIPPING, it's time to WAIT upon the Lord…

"But those who WAIT on the LORD shall renew their strength; they shall mount up with wings like eagles, they shall run and not be weary, they shall walk and not faint." **Isaiah 40:31 NKJV**

READ: **Psalm 116:1**
Pray for your:

Family:

_____
_____
_____
_____
_____
_____

Friends:

_____
_____
_____
_____
_____
_____

Community Group:

_____
_____
_____
_____
_____
_____

…………

REVELATION
the End

Church:

_____
_____
_____
_____
_____
_____

Nation:

_____
_____
_____
_____
_____
_____

Leaders:

_____
_____
_____
_____
_____
_____

Yourself:

_____
_____
_____
_____
_____
_____

. . . .

THURSDAY: WORK

After WAKING UP, WORSHIPPING the Lord, and WAITING upon the Lord, it's time to WORK...

"WORK hard so God can approve you. Be a good worker, one who does not need to be ashamed and who correctly explains the word of truth." **2 Timothy 2:15 NLT**

Fearless!
Read **Revelation 6**

In **Revelation 4** and **5** we get a glimpse of heaven and God in all His glory. We see the redeemed worshipping God, rejoicing in their salvation. It is a beautiful picture of God fulfilling His promise to protect his children from the Day of Judgment—**Revelation 3:10.** Christian, be fearless—**1 John 4:18**! You are covered by the blood of the Lamb. You are promised heaven! Walk confidently in your calling as a soldier for Christ! Battle for lost souls today, because judgment is coming for them tomorrow.

For in **Revelation 6**, we see what is to come to those who reject Jesus Christ as their Lord and Savior. We see the wrath of God poured out on sinful mankind in fierce judgment. We see the beginning of the Tribulation.

Here, John is in heaven watching Jesus break open the seals and he sees the destructive outcome each seal has on earth. The judgments are progressive in nature. For we not only serve a God of justice, but a God of love. Don't you think God would stop the judgments if all of mankind turned to Him in repentance? God wants people to repent. But He gives them the free will to choose. And they choose to reject Him; so with the opening of each seal the judgments increase in severity and intensity.

Four horsemen appear in the first four seals. The first seal – the rider

....

comes on a white horse, symbolizing peace. This is the calm before the storm. The rider is the Antichrist—**Matthew 24:3-5**. People will follow him, obsessed with the peace he offers, but it is a false peace that is short lived.

The opening of the second seal reveals the second horse: a red horse symbolizing war. The rider of this horse is also the Antichrist and God allows him the power to remove peace from the world and create war and violent slaughter everywhere—**Matthew 24:6-7**.

The third seal brings a black horse, symbolizing the famine that will take place due to the worldwide wars that have destroyed the food supply. There will be global hunger—**Matthew 24:7**.

When Jesus opens the fourth seal, a green (or pale) horse emerges, representing death. The rider on the horse is identified as Death and Hades and God gives him the power to bring to death 25 percent of the world's population.

As the fifth seal is opened, John sees under an altar the souls of believers who are martyred for their faith. These believers come to faith during the Tribulation period and are executed for their testimony. Here, these martyrs cry out to God asking when He will avenge their blood. And they are told to wait a little while longer. God will answer their prayers for vengeance in His timing.

Revelation 6 closes with the opening of the sixth seal. The sixth seal commences what the prophets in the Old Testament called the Day of the Lord—**Revelation 6:17, Joel 1-2**. It is God's divine wrath seen in overwhelming earthquakes and natural disasters. It prompts tremendous fear amongst the people on earth, as they cannot escape the terror. Finally they acknowledge the source of all their trouble: Jesus Christ, the Lamb. And yet, they still do not repent.

Christian, these judgments are terrifying and they are coming to those who reject Jesus Christ. Today is the day of salvation—**2 Corinthians 6:2**. Be fearless in your testimony. Share the gospel: Jesus Christ saves!

. . . .

Read **Hebrews 10:31.** Knowing what is going to happen during the Tribulation, why is it "a fearful thing to fall into the hands of the living God?"

_____
_____
_____
_____
_____
_____

Read **Genesis 6, 7:17-24.** How is the time of the Tribulation similar to what took place in Noah's day?

_____
_____
_____
_____
_____
_____

Read **Daniel 9:24-27.** What does Daniel say about the Antichrist?

_____
_____
_____
_____
_____
_____

Jesus told his disciples what was going to happen during the end times. Pick a verse in **Matthew 24,** and share why it is important.

_____
_____
_____
_____
_____
_____

Prayer: Father, thank You for sending Jesus Christ to die on the cross for my sins, saving me from the coming Tribulation.

. . . .

FRIDAY: WITNESS

After WAKING UP, WORSHIPPING the Lord, and WAITING

upon the Lord it's time to WORK...

> "But you shall receive power when the Holy Spirit has come upon
> you; and you shall be WITNESSES to Me...to the end of the earth."
> **Acts 1:8 NKJV**

Read **1 John 4:18, Joshua 1:9, 2 Timothy 1:7.** How are you going to
"be fearless" in your testimony today, proclaiming Jesus Christ to a
lost world?

_____

_____

_____

_____

_____

_____

How will you respond to the person who says they are going to wait a
little while longer before they receive Jesus Christ as their Lord and
Savior?

_____

_____

_____

_____

_____

_____

Read **Amos 4:12.** Examine your walk with God. Are you prepared to
meet God?

_____

_____

_____

_____

_____

_____

. . . .

With the opening of each seal in **Revelation 6**, we see God progressively judging the earth, awakening the people to their sin. Today, is God trying to get your attention about a sin in your life? Are you listening? Share.

_____

_____

_____

_____

_____

_____

Read **Revelation 6:9-11** and **Romans 12:19.** The opening of the fifth seal reveals an outpouring of persecution of Christians during the Tribulation, with God's promise to avenge the murder of His people. Have you been persecuted for your testimony and faith in Jesus Christ? Share.

_____

_____

_____

_____

_____

_____

Read **Ephesians 1:3-14.** When you are persecuted for your faith, it is important to remember the promises and blessings God gives His people. How have you experienced the favor of God in the midst of persecution?

_____

_____

_____

_____

_____

_____

Read **2 Peter 3:9.** God does not delight in the death of the wicked. He wants people to repent of their sin and respond to His free gift of salvation and His offer of forgiveness. But how will people hear about Jesus unless someone tells them — **Romans 10:14-15**? How is your community group going to share the gospel with the lost?

....

REVELATION
the End

Write your prayer:

. . . .

Week 14: Revelation 7:1-8

. . . .

MONDAY: WAKE UP

"WAKE UP, for the coming of our salvation is nearer now than when we first believed." **Romans 13:11 NLT**

Lord, please open my eyes to Your heart. Illuminate Your truths to me. Speak Lord, Your servant listens.

Read: **Revelation 7:1-8**

What does the verse say?

_____
_____
_____
_____
_____
_____

What is the lesson?

_____
_____
_____
_____
_____
_____

What is God telling you?

_____
_____
_____
_____

. . . .

_____

_____

What is your commitment?

_____

_____

_____

_____

_____

_____

. . . .

TUESDAY: WORSHIP

After WAKING UP, it's time to WORSHIP...

"But the hour is coming, and is now here, when the true worshippers will WORSHIP the Father in spirit and truth, for the Father is seeking such people to worship him." **John 4:23 ESV**

Lift High the Cross
George William Kitchin, 1887

Refrain:
Lift high the cross, the love of Christ proclaim
Till all the world adore His sacred name.

1 Come, Christians, follow where our Captain trod,
Our king victorious, Christ, the Son of God. [Refrain]

2 Led on their way by this triumphant sign,
The hosts of God in conqu'ring ranks combine. [Refrain]

3 All newborn soldiers of the Crucified
Bear on the brow the seal of Him who died. [Refrain]

4 O Lord, once lifted on the glorious tree,
As Thou hast promised, draw us all to Thee. [Refrain]

5 Let ev'ry race and ev'ry language tell
Of Him who saves our lives from death and hell. [Refrain]

6 So shall our song of triumph ever be;
Praise to the Crucified for victory! [Refrain]

Read **Matthew 16:24.** Explain this verse.

_____

_____

_____

....

_____
_____
_____

Read **Galatians 6:14.** What should we boast about? Why?

_____
_____
_____
_____
_____
_____

Read **Revelation 7:3.** What is the seal of God?

_____
_____
_____
_____
_____
_____

Explain why Christians can sing a "song of triumph."

_____
_____
_____
_____
_____
_____

Write your prayer:

_____
_____
_____
_____
_____
_____

. . . .

WEDNESDAY: WAIT

After WAKING UP, WORSHIPPING, it's time to WAIT upon the Lord...

"But those who WAIT on the LORD shall renew their strength; they shall mount up with wings like eagles, they shall run and not be weary, they shall walk and not faint." **Isaiah 40:31 NKJV**

READ: **Psalm 91**
Pray for your:

Family:

_____
_____
_____
_____
_____
_____

Friends:

_____
_____
_____
_____
_____
_____

Community Group:

_____
_____
_____
_____
_____
_____

. . . .

REVELATION
the End

Church:

_____
_____
_____
_____
_____
_____

Nation:

_____
_____
_____
_____
_____
_____

Leaders:

_____
_____
_____
_____
_____
_____

Yourself:

_____
_____
_____
_____
_____
_____

. . . .

THURSDAY: WORK

After WAKING UP, WORSHIPPING the Lord, and WAITING upon the Lord, it's time to WORK...

"WORK hard so God can approve you. Be a good worker, one who does not need to be ashamed and who correctly explains the word of truth." **2 Timothy 2:15 NLT**

God Protects His People
Read **Revelation 7:1-8**

Here in **Revelation 7** we see a break in the judgments that are being unleashed on earth. There is a pause. Four angels are standing at the corners of the earth, holding back the winds. Everything is calm. The leaves in the trees are not rustling; the sea is smooth as glass. It's as if the earth is holding its breath.

Then John sees an angel coming from the east, carrying the seal of the living God. He hears the angel call out to the four angels who are granted power to harm the earth, "Hold on! Don't hurt the land or the sea until we have placed God's seal of protection on His bondservants." 144,000 Jews are selected from the tribes of Israel. They are marked with God's seal and given a special ministry. These are the missionaries in the Tribulation, with a specific mission: proclaiming the gospel of Christ to a dying world.

The last verse of **Revelation 6** poises a question, "For the great day of His wrath has come, and who is able to stand?" The answer is found here in **Revelation 7.** The 144,000 will stand because they are protected by God. They will be the light during the dark night of the Tribulation, pointing people to Jesus. Though Israel failed in their witness during the Old Testament, they will impact the world during this time and many will be saved.

God will specifically choose these 144,000. He will give them gifts and anoint them for service. He has a plan and they play a strategic role in that plan. Christian, you too, are chosen by God — **Ephesians 1:1**. God says, "For I know the thoughts that I think toward you, thoughts of peace and not of evil to give you a future and a hope" — **Jeremiah 29:11**. God has called you to a special ministry. He has given you gifts to use for His glory. He has placed you where you are for such a time as this — **Esther 4:14**. God is strategic in His timing and you play a vital role in His plan. Are you ready to step it up for Him? Right now hear God whispering to your heart, "My seal is on you! I will protect you, so be bold in your testimony!"

Read **Revelation 7:3,** and **Ezekiel 9:3-4** (See also **Revelation 9:4, 14:1**). What is the seal of God? Explain.

_____

_____

_____

_____

_____

_____

The 144,000 Jews came from the twelve tribes of Israel. What does God say about the twelve tribes of Israel in **Genesis 49:1-27?**

_____

_____

_____

_____

_____

_____

In **Revelation 7:1-8,** we see God placing His seal of protection on the 144,000 Jews. Name another time in the Bible when God protected His people from judgment.

_____

_____

_____

_____

_____

_____

....

Read **Revelation 7:3, 1 Corinthians 7:22-23** and **Luke 17:10.** What is a bondservant?

_____

_____

_____

_____

_____

_____

What does **Revelation 7:1-8** reveal to you about God?

_____

_____

_____

_____

_____

_____

PRAYER: Thank You Lord for placing Your seal on me!

. . . .

FRIDAY: WITNESS

After WAKING UP, WORSHIPPING the Lord, WAITING upon

the Lord, and WORKING, it's time to WITNESS!

"But you shall receive power when the Holy Spirit has come upon you; and you shall be **witnesses** to Me...to the end of the earth." **Acts 1:8 NKJV**

Read **1 John 4:19.** Are you aware that God loves you personally? Share.

_____
_____
_____
_____
_____
_____

Read **Psalm 119:1-11.** Do you live out your faith boldly? Share.

_____
_____
_____
_____
_____
_____

Why do people refuse to believe the truth of Jesus Christ and the gospel message? Explain and share a verse.

_____
_____
_____
_____
_____
_____

Read **1 Corinthians 12:27-28, Ephesians 4:11-13, and Romans 12:6-8.** God gave the 144,000 a special ministry, to reach the lost with the

. . . .

gospel during the Tribulation period. God has given you a special ministry too! What has God called you to do? Share.

_____
_____
_____
_____
_____
_____

What special ministry is your community group called to do for the glory of God?

_____
_____
_____
_____
_____
_____

Read **Psalm 23.** After reading this Psalm, how are you encouraged to walk confidently in the calling God has given you?

_____
_____
_____
_____
_____
_____

Write your prayer:

_____
_____
_____
_____
_____
_____

....

REVELATION
the End

. . . .

Week 15: Revelation 7:9-17

. . . .

MONDAY: WAKE UP

"WAKE UP, for the coming of our salvation is nearer now than when we first believed." **Romans 13:11 NLT**

Lord, please open my eyes to Your heart. Illuminate Your truths to me.

Speak Lord, Your servant listens.

Read: **Revelation 7:9-17**

What does the verse say?

_____
_____
_____
_____
_____
_____

What is the lesson?

_____
_____
_____
_____
_____
_____

What is God telling you?

_____
_____
_____
_____
_____

. . . .

What is your commitment?

_____
_____
_____
_____
_____
_____
_____

TUESDAY: WORSHIP

After WAKING UP, it's time to WORSHIP…

"But the hour is coming, and is now here, when the true worshippers will WORSHIP the Father in spirit and truth, for the Father is seeking such people to worship him." **John 4:23 ESV**

How Bright These Glorious Spirits Shine!
Isaac Watts, 1707

How bright these glorious spirits shine!
Whence all their white array?
How came they to the blissful seats
Of everlasting day?
Lo! These are they from suff'rings great
Who came to realms of light!
And in the blood of Christ have washed
Those robes which shine so bright.

Now, with triumphal palms, they stand
Before the throne on high,
And serve the God they love, amidst
The glories of the sky.
His presence fills each heart with joy,
Tunes ev'ry mouth to sing:
By day, by night, the sacred courts
With glad hosannas ring.

Hunger and thirst are felt no more,
Nor suns with scorching ray;
God is their Sun, whose cheering beams
Diffuse eternal day.
The Lamb which dwells amidst the throne
Shall o'er them still preside,
Feed them with nourishment divine,
And all their footsteps guide.

…………

'Mong pastures green he'll lead his flock
Where living streams appear;
And God the Lord from ev'ry eye
Shall wipe off ev'ry tear.
To him who sits upon the throne,
The God whom we adore,
And to the Lamb that once was slain,
Be glory evermore!

Read **Revelation 7:9-17,** and **Psalm 100.**

How will we worship God in heaven?

_____
_____
_____
_____
_____
_____

Why do we sing and worship God today?

_____
_____
_____
_____
_____
_____

If someone were to ask you to write a couple lines to a worship song, based on **Revelation 7:9-17**, what would you write?

_____
_____
_____
_____
_____
_____

PRAYER: I adore You Lord!

. . . .

WEDNESDAY: WAIT

After WAKING UP, WORSHIPPING, it's time to WAIT upon the Lord…

"But those who WAIT on the LORD shall renew their strength; they shall mount up with wings like eagles, they shall run and not be weary, they shall walk and not faint." **Isaiah 40:31 NKJV**

READ: **Psalm 23:1-3**
Pray for your:

Family:

_____
_____
_____
_____
_____
_____

Friends:

_____
_____
_____
_____
_____
_____

Community Group:

_____
_____
_____
_____
_____
_____

…………

REVELATION
the End

Church:

_____
_____
_____
_____
_____
_____
_____

Nation:

_____
_____
_____
_____
_____
_____
_____

Leaders:

_____
_____
_____
_____
_____
_____
_____

Yourself:

_____
_____
_____
_____
_____
_____
_____

. . . .

THURSDAY: WORK

After WAKING UP, WORSHIPPING the Lord, and WAITING upon the Lord, it's time to WORK...

"WORK hard so God can approve you. Be a good worker, one who does not need to be ashamed and who correctly explains the word of truth." **2 Timothy 2:15 NLT**

God's Saving Grace Triumphs!
Read: **Revelation 7:9-17**

God does not give up on people. He wants people to escape the terror of eternity in hell. So here, in **Revelation 7**, we see that in the midst of God's wrath and judgment, His saving grace triumphs! The vast crowd of people standing before God's throne are the redeemed who come to Christ during the Tribulation. They get a second chance!

During the chaos of the Tribulation, a mass uprising takes place as the 144,000 evangelists preach the gospel—**Matthew 24:14**. Many people acknowledge Jesus Christ as their Lord and Savior, recognizing that He is the only way to God, and they are saved—**John 14:6**. God's grace is beautifully portrayed in this Great Awakening.

The Bible says that when one sinner accepts Jesus Christ as their Lord and Savior, there is a party amongst the angels in heaven—**Luke 15:10**. And that is what we see here, a party celebrating the greatness of God! All of the angels, the twenty-four elders, the four living beings, and the vast crowd of the redeemed are standing around the throne, marveling at how awesome God is; worshipping Him— **Revelation 7:11-13**.

Heaven is a place of joy; there are no more tears, broken hearts, pain, or sorrow—**Revelation 7:17**. God shelters His people, protecting them from danger—**Revelation 7:15-16**. And as their Shepherd, the Lamb, Jesus Christ, leads them—**Revelation 7:17**. Heaven is God's presence,

. . . .

a place of perfection. It's eternity with Jesus.

Today, the devil wants to keep you from living for heaven or from taking people with you. He tries to distract you with the things of this world. Christian where is your focus? On heaven? Or the world? The glory we will experience in heaven far outweighs the cares of this world — **2 Corinthians 4:16-18**. So live for heaven! Live for Jesus! God says, "today is the day of salvation" — **2 Corinthians 6:1**. Choose life!

Read **Revelation 7:10 Ephesians 2:4-9.** What does salvation mean?

_____
_____
_____
_____
_____
_____

Read **Romans 3:22-25, 5:9, Psalm 51:7,** and **Hebrews 10:19.** How are sinners made right in God's sight, able to stand in His holy presence?

_____
_____
_____
_____
_____
_____

Read **Revelation 7:12.** As the angels, the elders, and the four-living beings worshipped God, they acknowledged His attributes. List God's attributes. Why do they use these words to worship and honor God?

_____
_____
_____
_____
_____
_____

. . . .

Read **John 10:1-16,** and **Hebrews 13:20.** What does the Bible say about Jesus being our Shepherd? Explain.

_____
_____
_____
_____
_____
_____

After reading **Revelation 4, 5,** and **7:9-17,** describe heaven.

_____
_____
_____
_____
_____
_____

Prayer: Father, thank You for Your saving grace!

. . . .

FRIDAY: WITNESS

After WAKING UP, WORSHIPPING the Lord, and WAITING

upon the Lord it's time to WORK...

> "But you shall receive power when the Holy Spirit has come upon
> you; and you shall be WITNESSES to Me...to the end of the earth."
> **Acts 1:8 NKJV**

Read **Philippians 1:20-30** and **3:17-21.** If we are "citizens of heaven,"
what is our purpose here on earth? How are you living it out?

_____
_____
_____
_____
_____
_____

In heaven there won't be any more suffering! Why do we face trials
and difficulties here on earth? Explain and share a verse.

_____
_____
_____
_____
_____
_____

Read **2 Peter 3:18.** You will be with Jesus for eternity. So, today, how
are you going to grow in your knowledge of Him?

_____
_____
_____
_____
_____
_____

This "great multitude" of people in heaven, in **Revelation 7,** come to

. . . .

faith during the Tribulation. Prior to the Tribulation they reject Jesus Christ as their Lord and Savior, but God loves them so much that He gives them a second chance to repent and turn to Him before it is too late. Name a time when God gave you a second chance. Share a verse.

_____

_____

_____

_____

_____

_____

We will not struggle with fear in heaven because God is our shelter — **Revelation 7:15**. How does God protect us today and why is fear and worry a sin? Read **Psalm 23:4,** and **Psalm 56:3-4** (See also **Isaiah 41:10, Matthew 10:28,** and **2 Timothy 1:7**).

_____

_____

_____

_____

_____

_____

No one can deny the testimony of a transformed life. When you spend time with Jesus and live your life for Jesus it impacts others. Read **Acts 4:13** (See also **Acts 4:1-22**). Can people tell that you have been with Jesus? How?

_____

_____

_____

_____

_____

What motivates you to serve Jesus Christ? Share a verse.

_____

_____

_____

_____

_____

. . . .

the End

This week, how is your community group going to reach out to the lost with the message of the gospel?

_____
_____
_____
_____
_____
_____

PRAYER: Lord, thank You for the hope of heaven!

. . . .

Week 16: **Revelation 8:1-5**

. . . .

MONDAY: WAKE UP

"WAKE UP, for the coming of our salvation is nearer now than when we first believed." **Romans 13:11 NLT**

Lord, please open my eyes to Your heart. Illuminate Your truths to me.

Speak Lord, Your servant listens.

Read: **Revelation 8:1-5**

What does the verse say?

_____
_____
_____
_____
_____
_____

What is the lesson?

_____
_____
_____
_____
_____
_____

What is God telling you?

_____
_____
_____
_____
_____
_____

. . . .

What is your commitment?

_____

_____

_____

_____

_____

_____

_____

TUESDAY: WORSHIP

After WAKING UP, it's time to WORSHIP...

"But the hour is coming, and is now here, when the true worshippers will WORSHIP the Father in spirit and truth, for the Father is seeking such people to worship him." **John 4:23 ESV**

Sweet Hour of Prayer
William W. Walford, 1845

Sweet hour of prayer! Sweet hour of prayer!
That calls me from a world of care,
And bids me at my Father's throne
Make all my wants and wishes known.
In seasons of distress and grief,
My soul has often found relief,
And oft escaped the tempter's snare,
By thy return, sweet hour of prayer!

Sweet hour of prayer! Sweet hour of prayer!
The joys I feel, the bliss I share,
Of those whose anxious spirits burn
With strong desires for thy return!
With such I hasten to the place
Where God my Savior shows His face,
And gladly take my station there,
And wait for thee, sweet hour of prayer!

Sweet hour of prayer! Sweet hour of prayer!
Thy wings shall my petition bear
To Him whose truth and faithfulness
Engage the waiting soul to bless.
And since He bids me seek His face,
Believe His Word and trust His grace,
I'll cast on Him my every care,
And wait for thee, sweet hour of prayer!

....

Sweet hour of prayer! Sweet hour of prayer!
May I thy consolation share,
Till, from Mount Pisgah's lofty height,
I view my home and take my flight.
This robe of flesh I'll drop, and rise
To seize the everlasting prize,
And shout, while passing through the air,
"Farewell, farewell, sweet hour of prayer!"

Read **Acts 16:16-34.** Paul and Silas were in prison, but they still prayed and sang hymns to God. What happened next?

_____

_____

_____

_____

_____

_____

Can you say that your times of prayer are "sweet hours of prayer"? Explain.

_____

_____

_____

_____

_____

_____

How does prayer affect your worship?

_____

_____

_____

_____

_____

_____

PRAYER: Abba! Here I am — ready to serve You however You wish, as I wait for Christ's return.

. . . .

WEDNESDAY: WAIT

After WAKING UP, WORSHIPPING, it's time to WAIT upon the Lord…

"But those who WAIT on the LORD shall renew their strength; they shall mount up with wings like eagles, they shall run and not be weary, they shall walk and not faint." **Isaiah 40:31 NKJV**

READ: **James 5:15-16**
Pray for your:

Family:

_____
_____
_____
_____
_____
_____

Friends:

_____
_____
_____
_____
_____
_____

Community Group:

_____
_____
_____
_____
_____
_____

…………

REVELATION
the End

Church:

_____

_____

_____

_____

_____

_____

Nation:

_____

_____

_____

_____

_____

_____

Leaders:

_____

_____

_____

_____

_____

_____

Yourself:

_____

_____

_____

_____

_____

_____

. . . .

THURSDAY: WORK

After WAKING UP, WORSHIPPING the Lord, and WAITING

upon the Lord, it's time to WORK...

"WORK hard so God can approve you. Be a good worker, one who
does not need to be ashamed and who correctly explains the word of
truth." **2 Timothy 2:15 NLT**

Powerful Prayer
Read: **Revelation 8:1-5**

In heaven, John sees Jesus break the seventh seal. There is complete
silence for a half an hour as the reality of the horror to come sinks in.
The seven angels who stand before God receive the seven trumpets.
They wait for the right time to blow them; for each trumpet is a
specific judgment. Yes, judgment is coming to the nonbeliever.
Christian, do you care?

John then sees another angel with a gold incense burner come to the
altar. The angel mixes the quantity of incense with the prayers of
God's people and the smoke ascends to God. Then the angel takes the
incense burner and throws it down to earth. With thunder crashing
and lightening flashing, it's almost as if the Lord is saying, "And let
the games begin. If you do not repent of your evil ways, you will
experience My wrath!"

What we are facing today is a spiritual problem and the only way to
solve it is through prayer. Christian, God hears your prayers! God's
will in heaven becomes a reality on earth, due to the prayers of God's
people. Your prayers make a difference! Prayer is getting your heart
aligned with God's heart, and when that happens things begin to
move. It has been said that Satan trembles when he sees the weakest
saint upon its knees.

So, will you get on your knees, persevering in prayer? Crying out to

....

the Lord for a revival amongst your family, your church, your friends, your community group, and your nation? People need Jesus. They need to get back to church. And the church needs to wake up and rise up for Jesus Christ because our salvation is nearer now than when we first believed — **Romans 13:11**. Christ is coming back soon. Judgment is coming for the nonbeliever. Now is the time for a revival — **2 Peter 3:9**!

Read **Revelation 8:1** and **Psalm 76:8-9.** Why do you think there was "silence" in heaven after the seventh seal was broken?

_____

_____

_____

_____

_____

_____

Read **Revelation 8:3** and **Luke 1:8-20.** Zechariah burned incense in the Lord's presence, symbolizing the people's prayers ascending to God. What happened next?

_____

_____

_____

_____

_____

_____

Read **Matthew 6:9-13.** How does Jesus teach His disciples to pray?

_____

_____

_____

_____

_____

_____

In order to avoid judgment, we need a revival. How will there be a spiritual awakening amongst the people? Read **2 Chronicles 7:14.**

. . . .

_____
_____
_____
_____
_____
_____

Throughout his epistles, Paul gives us examples of prayers. How did Paul pray for the people in Colosse? Read **Colossians 1:9-14.**

_____
_____
_____
_____
_____
_____

PRAYER: Thank You Lord for hearing and answering my prayers!

. . . .

FRIDAY: WITNESS

After WAKING UP, WORSHIPPING the Lord, WAITING upon

the Lord, and WORKING, it's time to WITNESS!

> "But you shall receive power when the Holy Spirit has come upon
> you; and you shall be WITNESSES to Me...to the end of the earth."
> **Acts 1:8 NKJV**

Read **Revelation 8:1.** Have you ever sat in complete silence for a half
an hour? If so, what was it like?

_____

_____

_____

_____

_____

_____

Read **Psalm 27:8.** Share a time when the Lord called you to step away
from something and spend some time with Him in prayer.

_____

_____

_____

_____

_____

_____

Do you mourn over lost souls? If so, what are you and your
community group going to do about it? Read **Romans 10:14-15.**

_____

_____

_____

_____

_____

_____

What would you say to the person who says, "God doesn't hear my

. . . .

prayers"? Explain and share a verse.

_____

_____

_____

_____

_____

_____

Read **Acts 1:14** and **Acts 2:42-47.** The believers gathered together and prayed. In your community group, delegate someone to keep track of the specific prayer requests throughout the rest of the study on Revelation. This person's job will be to record the prayer requests and document how and when God answered the prayers, sharing the praise reports with the group.

_____

_____

_____

_____

_____

_____

What is your community group praying for? Include verses with your prayer requests.

_____

_____

_____

_____

_____

_____

Write your prayer:

_____

_____

_____

_____

_____

REVELATION
the End

....

Week 17: Revelation 8:6-9:21

. . . .

MONDAY: WAKE UP

"WAKE UP, for the coming of our salvation is nearer now than when we first believed." **Romans 13:11 NLT**

Lord, please open my eyes to Your heart. Illuminate Your truths to me.

Speak Lord, Your servant listens.

Read: **Revelation 8:6-9:21**

What does the verse say?

_____

_____

_____

_____

_____

_____

What is the lesson?

_____

_____

_____

_____

_____

_____

What is God telling you?

_____

_____

_____

_____

. . . .

REVELATION
the End

What is your commitment?

TUESDAY: WORSHIP

After WAKING UP, it's time to WORSHIP...

"But the hour is coming, and is now here, when the true worshippers will WORSHIP the Father in spirit and truth, for the Father is seeking such people to worship him." **John 4:23 ESV**

A Mighty Fortress is Our God
Martin Luther, 1529

A mighty fortress is our God,
A bulwark never failing;
Our helper he, amid the flood
Of mortal ills prevailing.
For still our ancient foe
Does seek to work us woe;
His craft and power are great,
And armed with cruel hate,
On earth is not his equal.

Did we in our strength confide,
Our striving would be losing,
Were not the right Man on our side,
The Man of God's own choosing.
You ask who that may be?
Christ Jesus, it is he;
Lord Sabaoth his name,
From age to age the same;
And he must win the battle.
And though this world, with devils filled,
Should threaten to undo us,
We will not fear, for God has willed
His truth to triumph through us.
The prince of darkness grim,
We tremble not for him;
His rage we can endure,
For lo! His doom is sure;

....

One little word shall fell him.

That Word above all earthly powers
No thanks to them abideth;
The Spirit and the gifts are ours
Through him who with us sideth.
Let goods and kindred go,
This mortal life also;
The body they may kill:
God's truth abideth still;
His kingdom is forever!

How is God "A mighty fortress"?

_____
_____
_____
_____
_____
_____

Read **Psalm 31.** David is crying out to the Lord in prayer. Name the problems David is facing?

_____
_____
_____
_____
_____

God protects His people, so even amidst his problems David praises the Lord. What does David say?

_____
_____
_____
_____
_____

Do you praise the Lord when you are facing trials? Explain.

. . . .

Write your prayer:

. . . .

WEDNESDAY: WAIT

After WAKING UP, WORSHIPPING, it's time to WAIT upon the Lord…

"But those who WAIT on the LORD shall renew their strength; they shall mount up with wings like eagles, they shall run and not be weary, they shall walk and not faint." **Isaiah 40:31 NKJV**

READ: **Matthew 3:8, Acts 3:19**
Pray for your:

Family:

_____
_____
_____
_____
_____
_____

Friends:

_____
_____
_____
_____
_____
_____

Community Group:

_____
_____
_____
_____
_____
_____

. . . .

W E E K *SEVENTEEN*

Church:

_____
_____
_____
_____
_____
_____

Nation:

_____
_____
_____
_____
_____
_____

Leaders:

_____
_____
_____
_____
_____
_____

Yourself:

_____
_____
_____
_____
_____
_____

. . . .

THURSDAY: WORK

After WAKING UP, WORSHIPPING the Lord, and WAITING upon the Lord, it's time to WORK...

"WORK hard so God can approve you. Be a good worker, one who does not need to be ashamed and who correctly explains the word of truth." **2 Timothy 2:15 NLT**

God's Wrath Unleashed!
Read: **Revelation 8:6-9:21**

Christian, God loves you! Today, will you rejoice over the fact that He has saved you from the destruction of hell and the torment of judgment? As His child, you are protected. You are marked and sealed — **Ephesians 1:13** and **Revelation 9:4**. No weapon formed against you shall prosper — **Isaiah 54:17**. But this promise is only for the believer, the person who has put their faith and trust in Jesus Christ. The nonbeliever, will face judgment unless they repent today and turn toward the Lord — **Ezekiel 18:23, 32**!

Here in **Revelation 8** and **9,** we see John in heaven watching the seven angels sound the seven trumpet judgments. The first four angels step forward and, in succession, blow their trumpets destroying the earth. The people on earth cannot escape the destruction. They cannot hide. Many are killed.

Then the fifth angel steps forward and blows his trumpet and a star that had fallen to the earth is given a key to the shaft of the bottomless pit. This star could very well be Satan — **Isaiah 14** and **Luke 10:18**. The bottomless pit is opened and locusts come out and descend upon the earth. These locusts are able to inflict physical pain on everyone but the people marked with the seal of God — **Revelation 9:4**. This is like a demonic annihilation of humanity. There is no relief from the torment. People seek death, trying to escape the pain and misery, but they cannot die.

....

Then the sixth angel blows his trumpet, and a voice speaks from the altar that stands in the presence of God. This voice calls out for the sixth angel to release the four angels who had been prepared for this very day. These four angels are demons; they are fallen angels who are turned loose to kill one-third of the remaining people on earth. So many people have now died, due to sinful rebellion.

God's wrath has been unleashed, and it's said that around 2 billion people will have died up to this point; but people still do not repent — **Revelation 9:21**. Christian, punishment does not always bring about repentance. These people have hardened their hearts to the voice of the Lord, to their own detriment. "Today, if you will hear His voice, do not harden your hearts as in the rebellion" — **Hebrews 3:15**. God loves you so much that He allows you to choose: life or death. Repent of your sin and choose life — **Deuteronomy 30:19b**!

Describe the first four trumpets.

_____
_____
_____
_____
_____
_____

Read **Revelation 9** and **Joel 2.** How do these two chapters compare to one another? Explain.

_____
_____
_____
_____
_____
_____

What is the "bottomless pit"? Read **Revelation 9:1-2, 11 (**See also: **Revelation 11:7; 17:8; 20:1).**

_____
_____
_____

. . . .

the End

_____

_____

_____

What actions described in **Revelation 9:20-21** are forbidden in the 10 Commandments found in **Exodus 20:2-17?** Explain.

_____

_____

_____

_____

_____

Read **Ephesians 6:10-17.** What is the armor of God, and why do Christians need it?

_____

_____

_____

_____

_____

Prayer: Father, thank You for sealing me with the Holy Spirit, protecting me from the evil in this world.

. . . .

FRIDAY: WITNESS

After WAKING UP, WORSHIPPING the Lord, and WAITING upon the Lord it's time to WORK...

> "But you shall receive power when the Holy Spirit has come upon you; and you shall be WITNESSES to Me...to the end of the earth."
> **Acts 1:8 NKJV**

Have you ever said, "I know the Bible says this, but..."? Share and include a verse.

_____
_____
_____
_____
_____
_____

Will you live your life like you are in a life or death battle for the souls of men and women/boys and girls? Explain.

_____
_____
_____
_____
_____
_____

Read **Hebrews 10:26-27.** Explain these verses.

_____
_____
_____
_____
_____

Read **1 John 1:9.** What sins do you need to confess?

_____
_____

....

_____
_____
_____
_____

Read **Ephesians 6:18.** Why does God call us to pray for "all Christians everywhere"?

_____
_____
_____
_____
_____
_____

"And they did not repent" — **Revelation 9:20**. If someone does not repent after they have been punished for a sin, what does that show about their true heart condition? Explain.

_____
_____
_____
_____
_____
_____

Who are you going to share the gospel with this week?

_____
_____
_____
_____
_____
_____

PRAYER: Abba! Thank You for correcting my wrong thoughts by directing me to Your Words of truth. I want to think rightly.

. . . .

Week 18: Revelation 10 & 11

. . . .

MONDAY: WAKE UP

"WAKE UP, for the coming of our salvation is nearer now than when we first believed." **Romans 13:11 NLT**

Lord, please open my eyes to Your heart. Illuminate Your truths to me.

Speak Lord, Your servant listens.

Read: **Revelation 10 & 11**

What does the verse say?

_____
_____
_____
_____
_____
_____

What is the lesson?

_____
_____
_____
_____
_____
_____

What is God telling you?

_____
_____
_____
_____
_____

. . . .

What is your commitment?

_____
_____
_____
_____
_____
_____
_____

. . . .

TUESDAY: WORSHIP

After WAKING UP, it's time to WORSHIP...

"But the hour is coming, and is now here, when the true worshippers will WORSHIP the Father in spirit and truth, for the Father is seeking such people to worship him." **John 4:23 ESV**

Near The End
Wm. G. Schell, 1897

Time moves on with solemn footsteps
As it nears the final shore;
Fast the sun of earth is sinking,
Soon our world shall be no more.
The sixth trumpet now is sounding
To prepare the holy bride —
Many on the golden altar,
"Purified, made white, and tried."

Lo! The angel now is standing
On the sea and on the land;
How His voice the air is rending,
As to God He lifts His hand!
What an awful, awful message!
Help us, Lord, this truth to see;
When the seventh trumpet thunders,
Then shall time no longer be.

One more trumpet yet to summon
Us before the judgment seat,
Then the time of our frail planet
Will be said to be complete.
How the wicked will be wailing,
And the righteous overjoyed,
When with fire the heav'ns are burning,
And the earth shall be destroyed.
While false prophets are confiding

....

In a foolish, erring dream
Of millennial enjoyments,
They neglect the cleansing stream.
Oh, poor sinner, don't believe them,
There will be no age to come;
If in life you find not Jesus,
Death will seal your awful doom.

How does the gospel affect your worship? Read **Romans 5:6-11.**

Is worship self-focused or God-focused? Why? List some questions you have about worshipping God.

Why are explanations of scripture set to song, powerful?

PRAYER: Thank You for opening my eyes to Jesus in my midst!

WEDNESDAY: WAIT

After WAKING UP, WORSHIPPING, it's time to WAIT upon the Lord…

"But those who WAIT on the LORD shall renew their strength; they shall mount up with wings like eagles, they shall run and not be weary, they shall walk and not faint." **Isaiah 40:31 NKJV**

READ: **Ecclesiastes 3:1, 7-8**
Pray for your:

Family:

_____
_____
_____
_____
_____
_____

Friends:

_____
_____
_____
_____
_____
_____

Community Group:

_____
_____
_____
_____
_____
_____

. . . .

REVELATION
the End

Church:

_____
_____
_____
_____
_____
_____

Nation:

_____
_____
_____
_____
_____
_____

Leaders:

_____
_____
_____
_____
_____
_____

Yourself:

_____
_____
_____
_____
_____
_____

. . . .

THURSDAY: WORK

After WAKING UP, WORSHIPPING the Lord, and WAITING upon the Lord, it's time to WORK...

"WORK hard so God can approve you. Be a good worker, one who does not need to be ashamed and who correctly explains the word of truth." **2 Timothy 2:15 NLT**

For God's Glory
Read: **Revelation 10** and **11**

We see a break between the sixth and seventh judgment in **Revelation 10:1** through **11:14.** God is so faithful! He knows breaks encourage, comfort, and strengthen His people when they are in the middle of chaos and struggle. God knows our frame—**Psalm 103:14**. He alone knows how much we can take, and He never gives us more than we can handle—**1 Corinthians 10:13**.

In **Revelation 11,** we see God using two witnesses, whom He raises up and prepares for this specific ministry—humbly sharing His truth to a dying world for three and half years of the Tribulation. These two prophets are lights igniting a revival amongst the people. Confident in God's calling on their life, His presence with them, and His supernatural protection of them—**Revelation 11:4-6**, they fearlessly proclaim the need for repentance and God's coming wrath and judgment for the rebellious. Many come to faith in Jesus Christ—**Revelation 14:12-13**, and yet many still refuse to surrender to the truth—**Revelation 11:10**. But these prophets remain faithful to their calling, humble before God—powerful before men.

Only when the prophets' testimonies are complete, their job ministering to the people done, does God allow Antichrist to rise up and kill them while the whole world watches—**Revelation 11:7-8**. Christian, no one can stop you from doing what God has called you to do! Remain faithful—**1 Timothy 1:19**. Fear God, not man—**Proverbs 29:25**!

....

The prophets' deaths are mocked. Evil appears to have won. But after three days the prophets rise from the dead and ascend to heaven, while their enemies watch. And in that same hour an earthquake kills 7,000 people. People are terrified and give glory to God — **Revelation 11:11-13**.

Christian, it is not over until God says it is over. If you claim to be a witness of Jesus Christ, people will look to your actions, not your words, to see the Truth. God often allows His kids to be placed into the fire of adversity, as it allows a sweet opportunity for one to give a silent witness of His glory, as it is reflected through Christ-like actions.

God loves you and what your facing right now is for His glory — **Psalm 50:15**! Rest assured, He will send for you when He needs you. God highly values one soul, and He knows your testimony is the very tool to impact someone's life.

Read **Revelation 10:4**. God's voice is frequently associated with thunder. Read **Psalm 29:3-9.** What does the Bible say about God's voice?

_____
_____
_____
_____
_____
_____

Why is the Word of God bittersweet? Read **Revelation 10:9-10,** and **Psalm 19:7-11** (See also: **Ezekiel 3:1-14**).

_____
_____
_____
_____
_____
_____

Read **Malachi 4:5-6** (See also: **1 Kings 17:1, 1 Kings 18:42-46, 2 Kings 1:10, 12** and **2 Kings 2:11-12**). Who might one of the witnesses be?

. . . .

_____
_____
_____
_____
_____
_____

Read **Matthew 17:3** (See also: **Exodus 7:17-21, and Deuteronomy 18:15-18).** Who might the other witness be?

_____
_____
_____
_____

Read **Acts 1:8** and **1 Peter 3:15.** A witness is a person who speaks the truth about Jesus Christ. What truths should Christians share when asked to give a defense for their faith in Jesus Christ? Include verses.

_____
_____
_____
_____

What rewards are promised to believers? Read **Revelation 11:18** (See also: **Mark 10:29-31, James 1:12,** and **1 Peter 5:4).**

_____
_____
_____
_____

Read **Hebrews 4:12-16.** Explain how the Word of God is "living and powerful."

_____
_____
_____

....

_____

_____

_____

There are many prophecies in Scripture. What God says will happen, will happen. What prophecy was given in **Amos 9:14-15**, and what year was it fulfilled?

_____

_____

_____

_____

_____

_____

PRAYER: Thank You Lord for giving me many opportunities to proclaim Your name and reach out to the lost, for Your glory!

. . . .

FRIDAY: WITNESS

After WAKING UP, WORSHIPPING the Lord, WAITING upon the Lord, and WORKING, it's time to WITNESS!

"But you shall receive power when the Holy Spirit has come upon you; and you shall be WITNESSES to Me...to the end of the earth."
Acts 1:8 NKJV

Read **Revelation 11:1-14.** Are you willing to endure persecution to reconcile men to God?

_____
_____
_____
_____
_____
_____

Do you believe God's grace changes hearts? Explain.

_____
_____
_____
_____
_____
_____

"Flight into the invisible is a denial of the call. A community of Jesus which seeks to hide itself has ceased to follow him."[2] Read **Matthew 5:14-16.** Explain this quote.

_____
_____
_____
_____
_____
_____

The two witnesses shared truth with the people in sin. Is there a specific sin you are struggling with? Read **1 John 1:9** and **Ezekiel 36:26-27.**

_____
_____
_____
_____
_____
_____

How do Christians reflect God's glory when they face opposition? Share a verse.

_____
_____
_____
_____
_____
_____

Read **1 Timothy 2:13.** Describe a time in your life when you recognized that "God's timing is perfect."

_____
_____
_____
_____
_____
_____

Read **1 Peter 4:10** (see also: **Romans 12:6-8).** What spiritual gifts do the people in your community group have? How are you all going to use your spiritual gifts to build community in your group?

_____
_____
_____
_____
_____
_____

PRAYER: Thank You Abba for standing with me in the flame!

. . . .

Week 19: Revelation 12

. . . .

MONDAY: WAKE UP

"WAKE UP, for the coming of our salvation is nearer now than when we first believed." **Romans 13:11 NLT**

Lord, please open my eyes to Your heart. Illuminate Your truths to me.

Speak Lord, Your servant listens.

Read: **Revelation 12**

What does the verse say?

_____
_____
_____
_____
_____
_____

What is the lesson?

_____
_____
_____
_____
_____

What is God telling you?

_____
_____
_____
_____
_____

. . . .

What is your commitment?

_____

_____

_____

_____

_____

_____

_____

TUESDAY: WORSHIP

After WAKING UP, it's time to WORSHIP...

"But the hour is coming, and is now here, when the true worshippers will WORSHIP the Father in spirit and truth, for the Father is seeking such people to worship him." **John 4:23 ESV**

Give Me The Wings Of Faith To Rise
Isaac Watts, 1709

Give us the wings of faith to rise
Within the veil, and see
The saints above, how great their joys,
How bright their glories be.

Once they were mourning here below,
Their couch was wet with tears;
They wrestled hard, as we do now,
With sins and doubts and fears.

We ask them whence their victory came:
They, with united breath,
Ascribe their conquest to the Lamb,
Their triumph to his death.

They marked the footsteps that he trod,
His zeal inspired their breast,
And, following their incarnate God,
Possess the promised rest.

Our glorious Leader claims our praise
For his own pattern given;
While the long cloud of witnesses
Show the same path to heaven.

Why is your hope found in Jesus Christ? Share a verse.

....

REVELATION
the End

_____
_____
_____
_____
_____
_____

Why is the Resurrection of Jesus Christ important? Read **1 Corinthians 15:3-8, 12-20** (see also: **Romans 4:24-25, Acts 5:30-31**).

_____
_____
_____
_____
_____
_____

How does Jesus Christ's resurrection impact your relationship with Him? How does it direct your worship?

_____
_____
_____
_____
_____
_____

Write down a line in a worship song that has been ministering to your heart and explain why it has impacted you.

_____
_____
_____
_____
_____
_____

PRAYER: King! I worship You and You alone.

. . . .

WEDNESDAY: WAIT

After WAKING UP, WORSHIPPING, it's time to WAIT upon the Lord…

"But those who WAIT on the LORD shall renew their strength; they shall mount up with wings like eagles, they shall run and not be weary, they shall walk and not faint." **Isaiah 40:31 NKJV**

READ: **Isaiah 54:15-17**
Pray for your:

Family:

_____
_____
_____
_____
_____
_____

Friends:

_____
_____
_____
_____
_____
_____

Community Group:

_____
_____
_____
_____
_____
_____

. . . .

REVELATION
the End

Church:

_____
_____
_____
_____
_____
_____

Nation:

_____
_____
_____
_____
_____
_____

Leaders:

_____
_____
_____
_____
_____
_____

Yourself:

_____
_____
_____
_____
_____
_____

. . . .

THURSDAY: WORK

After WAKING UP, WORSHIPPING the Lord, and WAITING upon the Lord, it's time to WORK...

"WORK hard so God can approve you. Be a good worker, one who does not need to be ashamed and who correctly explains the word of truth." **2 Timothy 2:15 NLT**

Truth Defeats Satan
Read: **Revelation 12**

In **Revelation 12**, John describes a significant event he witnessed. He saw a pregnant woman clothed with the sun, with the moon beneath her feet and a crown of twelve stars on her head—**Revelation 12:1**, representing Israel—**Genesis 37:9-11, Isaiah 26:17-18**.

He sees another event where a red dragon, representing Satan, falls from heaven taking one-third of the angels with him to the earth—**Isaiah 14:12, Ezekiel 28:11**. John then sees Satan standing before the woman ready to devour her baby as soon as it is born—**Revelation 12:4**. The baby represents Jesus Christ, the Messiah. From the beginning Satan has been trying to destroy Israel and stop God's work of redemption found in His only Son, Jesus Christ. But his plan is thwarted every time—**Revelation 12:5-6**.

Then a war breaks out in heaven, and Michael the archangel and the angels under his command fight Satan and his demons. Satan loses the battle and is forced out of heaven, thrown to the earth—**Revelation 12:7-10**. Satan's power is broken. This event is huge! Because when Satan was first thrown out of heaven, due to his pride—**Isaiah 14:12**, he was still allowed access to heaven. And he would accuse Christians before God—**Job 1:6**. But after this event, Satan can no longer enter God's presence to accuse Christians!

Christian, have you ever been accused of doing something wrong?

....

That is what Satan does night and day; he accuses Christians. He tries to tear them down and destroy their reputations. Satan seeks to hinder the work God is doing through them. But know this, if you are a genuine Christian, Jesus Christ is your Advocate—**1 John 2:1, Hebrews 7:25**. Jesus is defending you. And He always wins.

Christian, you are able to defeat Satan and his false accusations because of Jesus Christ, who is Truth—**John 14:6**. No lie can stand in His presence because He is perfect in knowledge—**Proverbs 12:19**. If you have not done anything wrong, the accusation will fade as you grow strong. "The righteous keep moving forward and those with clean hands become stronger and stronger"—**Job 17:9 NLT**. When you do sin, and Satan condemns you, realize the grace and redemption found in the cross and Jesus Christ's resurrection. Jesus Christ's shed blood on the cross covers all of your sins past, present and future—**Revelation 12:11, Hebrews 9:22**. No charge can stand against you—**Romans 8:33-39**! Jesus paid for it all! So, walk in integrity and truth. "Be of good cheer; your sins are forgiven you"—**Matthew 9:2 NKJV**.

Know this—you also overcome Satan by the power of your testimony—**Revelation 12:11**. Invade enemy territory by sharing the gospel and its impact on your life. When you proclaim Christ to others, and His work in your life, you further His Kingdom here on earth; as people witness tangible evidence of God's saving transformative power! No one can argue with your testimony.

Satan knows he has little time left, and he wants to take as many people down as he can. So, in **Revelation 12:12-17**, he increases his efforts to destroy Israel. However, God protects Israel for three and a half years. Satan then turns his rage on every Christian walking the earth during the Tribulation.

Persecutions will increase, but Christian no one can take your salvation from you. No one can take Christ's presence from your life. You have this assurance—**Romans 8:38-39, John 3:36**. So, having the right attitude while persecuted is key. Remember Paul, he said, "For to me, living is for Christ, and dying is even better. What has happened to me here has helped spread the Good News"—**Philippians 1:21, 1:12**.

....

Read **Matthew 2:13-18.** Which ruler did Satan use, in his attempt to kill baby Jesus?

_____

_____

_____

_____

_____

_____

Why has Satan been trying to destroy Jesus from the very beginning of time? Explain and share a verse.

_____

_____

_____

_____

_____

_____

Read **Revelation 12:7-8, Daniel 10:13, and Jude 9**. What is going on in heaven?

_____

_____

_____

_____

_____

_____

Read **Revelation 12:11, Hebrews 9:22** and **1 John 1:7.** What is the significance of the "blood of the Lamb"? Explain.

_____

_____

_____

_____

_____

_____

PRAYER: Thank You Jesus for defending me against Satan's false accusations.

. . . .

FRIDAY: WITNESS

After WAKING UP, WORSHIPPING the Lord, WAITING upon

the Lord, and WORKING, it's time to WITNESS!

"But you shall receive power when the Holy Spirit has come upon you; and you shall be **witnesses** to Me...to the end of the earth." **Acts 1:8 NKJV**

Read **Hebrews 13:6.** How has God shown you that He is with you always?

_____

_____

_____

_____

_____

_____

Obedience to God and His Word characterizes a genuine Christian. Read **1 Thessalonians 5:12-13**, and **Hebrews 13:17.** How are we to honor and respect the spiritual leaders God has placed in our lives?

_____

_____

_____

_____

_____

_____

Describe different ways Satan tries to deceive us. What should we do? Share a verse.

_____

_____

_____

_____

_____

_____

. . . .

Read **Revelation 12:10-11.** Satan is called the Accuser. He is the one who accuses us before God. Have you ever been accused of doing something you didn't do? Describe what happened.

_____

_____

_____

_____

_____

_____

Read **Ephesians 6:12.** How are you going to live this verse out when you face opposition?

_____

_____

_____

_____

_____

_____

How has God moved powerfully in your life? Share your testimony.

_____

_____

_____

_____

_____

_____

Read 1 Thessalonians 5:14. How is your community group going to encourage those who are timid in their faith?

_____

_____

_____

_____

_____

_____

PRAYER: Father! Thank You for Your Word. It gives me strength to face the enemy's opposition.

. . . .

REVELATION
the End

. . . .

Week 20: **Revelation 13**

. . . .

MONDAY: WAKE UP

"WAKE UP, for the coming of our salvation is nearer now than when we first believed." **Romans 13:11 NLT**

Lord, please open my eyes to Your heart. Illuminate Your truths to me. Speak Lord, Your servant listens.

Read: **Revelation 13**

What does the verse say?

_____
_____
_____
_____
_____
_____

What is the lesson?

_____
_____
_____
_____
_____
_____

What is God telling you?

_____
_____
_____
_____
_____

. . . .

What is your commitment?

_____
_____
_____
_____
_____
_____
_____

TUESDAY: WORSHIP

After WAKING UP, it's time to WORSHIP...

"But the hour is coming, and is now here, when the true worshippers will WORSHIP the Father in spirit and truth, for the Father is seeking such people to worship him." **John 4:23 ESV**

When I Survey the Wondrous Cross
Issac Watts, 1707

When I survey the wondrous cross
On which the Prince of glory died,
My richest gain I count but loss,
And pour contempt on all my pride.

Forbid it, Lord, that I should boast,
Save in the death of Christ my God!
All the vain things that charm me most,
I sacrifice them to His blood.

See from His head, His hands, His feet,
Sorrow and love flow mingled down!
Did e'er such love and sorrow meet,
Or thorns compose so rich a crown?

His dying crimson, like a robe,
Spreads o'er His body on the tree;
Then I am dead to all the globe,
And all the globe is dead to me.

Were the whole realm of nature mine,
That were a present far too small;
Love so amazing, so divine,
Demands my soul, my life, my all.

Read **1 Corinthians 2:2.** Why is the gospel important?

....

Read **Psalm 34:2.** Why should those that are discouraged "take heart"?

Jesus Christ is truth—**John 14:6**. Antichrist is false—**Daniel 7:21-26**. How are you going to share the truth with your family and friends this week?

This week, how are you going to worship Jesus Christ in spirit and in truth—**John 4:23**?

PRAYER: Thank You for Your perfect love!

WEDNESDAY: WAIT

After WAKING UP, WORSHIPPING, it's time to WAIT upon the Lord…

"But those who WAIT on the LORD shall renew their strength; they shall mount up with wings like eagles, they shall run and not be weary, they shall walk and not faint." **Isaiah 40:31 NKJV**

READ: **Jude 20-25**
Pray for your:

Family:

_____
_____
_____
_____
_____
_____

Friends:

_____
_____
_____
_____
_____
_____

Community Group:

_____
_____
_____
_____
_____
_____

. . . .

REVELATION
the End

Church:

_____
_____
_____
_____
_____
_____

Nation:

_____
_____
_____
_____
_____
_____

Leaders:

_____
_____
_____
_____
_____
_____

Yourself:

_____
_____
_____
_____
_____
_____

. . . .

THURSDAY: WORK

After WAKING UP, WORSHIPPING, it's time to WAIT upon the Lord!

"WORK hard so God can approve you. Be a good worker, one who does not need to be ashamed and who correctly explains the word of truth." **2 Timothy 2:15 NLT**

The Unholy Trinity
Read: **Revelation 13**

In John's vision, he witnesses a beast, the Antichrist, rising up out of the sea, the abyss where the demons inhabit. He sees this beast as the final powerful world ruler; as Satan, gives Antichrist his own power and authority — **Revelation 13:1-2**.

See, Satan has his own imitation of the holy Trinity. The holy Trinity is God the Father, the Son, and Holy Spirit. But Satan's unholy Trinity is Satan (in the place of God), Antichrist (in the place of Jesus Christ), and the False Prophet (in the place of the Holy Spirit). Satan has always wanted to be like God — **Isaiah 14:14**, so he tries to deceive the people into believing he has the same power. But he doesn't. There is a day when Satan will be no more — **Revelation 20**.

In **Revelation 13**, the Antichrist appears to be wounded beyond recovery, and is supposedly resurrected. This, however, is a fake death and resurrection as he deceptively tries to mimic the real Christ. But the people believe it and stand in awe of Antichrist; they worship him and follow him unquestioningly — **Revelation 13:3-4, 2 Thessalonians 2:9**. The next beast is the False Prophet. The False Prophet's goal is to point people to Antichrist and the worship of Satan. So, the False Prophet performs signs and miracles and gets people to believe the lies. He then places a statue of Antichrist in the temple and commands the people to worship it as if it were God — **Revelation 13:11-15**. This is exactly what Satan wants! He has always coveted the worship of God for himself — **Isaiah 14:12-15**. But the

....

names of these people, worshiping Satan, will not be found in the Book of Life, they will not go to heaven — they are going to hell — **Revelation 13:8**.

So, God allows Antichrist authority over the earth to do what he wants for the last three and a half years of the Tribulation. Antichrist blasphemes God, slandering God's holy name and His people that are in heaven. He slanders anything that has to do with God — **Revelation 13:5-7**. Christian, has your name ever been slandered? Slander sticks around for a long time. Once lies are circulated amongst a group of people, it is really difficult to clear a person's name and reputation. So, Christian, don't do it! When you slander someone you partner with Satan and his desire to tear down God, His saints, and His Kingdom.

Christianity is not a leisure stroll. It is a constant fight. And it will be very difficult for the Christians during the Tribulation, as they will face the fiercest persecution imaginable for believing in Jesus Christ — **Revelation 13:9-10**. But Christian, God will not let evil win! Endure to the end — **Mark 13:13**.

The beast in **Revelation 13** is the Antichrist. What does the Bible say about Antichrist? Read **Daniel 7:21-26, Daniel 8:8:23-25, 2 Thessalonians 2:3-11** (See also: **Daniel 9:24-27, Daniel 11:36-45**).

_____

_____

_____

_____

_____

_____

The last 3 ½ years of the Tribulation begins with the abomination of desolation. What is the "abomination of desolation"? Read **Revelation 13:14-15, Daniel 9:24-27, Daniel 11:31** (See also: **Matthew 24:15, 2 Thessalonians 2:3-4**).

_____

_____

_____

_____

_____

. . . .

Read **1 John 2:18-29, 1 John 4:2-3, 2 John 7.** Here John mentions the coming world ruler Antichrist, but he also labels the false teachers in the world today as "antichrists." What are the differences between true genuine Christians and antichrists?

_____
_____
_____
_____
_____
_____

Read **Revelation 13:8,** and **Luke 10:20.** What does it mean to have your name written in the Book of Life?

_____
_____
_____
_____
_____
_____

Read **Matthew 24:24.** Do signs and miracles always come from God?

_____
_____
_____
_____
_____
_____

Read **Revelation 13:16-18.** What is the mark of the beast?

_____
_____
_____
_____
_____
_____

PRAYER: Jesus, thank you for being the true and living God!

. . . .

FRIDAY: WITNESS

After WAKING UP, WORSHIPPING the Lord, WAITING upon the Lord, and WORKING, it's time to WITNESS!

> "But you shall receive power when the Holy Spirit has come upon you; and you shall be WITNESSES to Me...to the end of the earth."
> **Acts 1:8 NKJV**

Read **1 John 2:12-14.** Is God's word living in your heart? Explain.

_____
_____
_____
_____
_____
_____

Read **John 2:17,** and **Psalm 69:9.** Does passion for God's house burn within you? Explain and share a verse.

_____
_____
_____
_____
_____
_____

Will you fight for the honor and virtue of God's people? Explain and share a verse.

_____
_____
_____
_____
_____
_____

How do you accept persecution and suffering with patience, endurance, perseverance, and faith? Read **2 Corinthians 10:4-5,** and **1 Peter 2:19-24.**

. . . .

_____
_____
_____
_____
_____

The Antichrist will blaspheme God's name and slander God's holy people. Are your words building up the people in your community group or are your words tearing them down? Explain and share a verse.

_____
_____
_____
_____
_____

Is there anything that will cause you to deny Jesus Christ?

_____
_____
_____
_____
_____

How is your community group going to walk in holiness, honoring God's name, when you live in a world that constantly blasphemes God?

_____
_____
_____
_____
_____

Read **Proverbs 29:18**. What vision is the Lord giving you for your community group?

_____
_____

....

Write your prayer:

. . . .

Week 21: Revelation 14

. . . .

MONDAY: WAKE UP

"WAKE UP, for the coming of our salvation is nearer now than when we first believed." **Romans 13:11 NLT**

Lord, please open my eyes to Your heart. Illuminate Your truths to me. Speak Lord, Your servant listens.

Read: **Revelation 14**

What does the verse say?

_____
_____
_____
_____
_____
_____

What is the lesson?

_____
_____
_____
_____
_____

What is God telling you?

_____
_____
_____
_____
_____

. . . .

What is your commitment?

_____

_____

_____

_____

_____

_____

. . . .

TUESDAY: WORSHIP

After WAKING UP, it's time to WORSHIP…

"But the hour is coming, and is now here, when the true worshippers will WORSHIP the Father in spirit and truth, for the Father is seeking such people to worship him." **John 4:23 ESV**

Redeemed
Fanny Crosby, 1882

Redeemed, how I love to proclaim it!
Redeemed by the blood of the Lamb;
Redeemed through His infinite mercy,
His child forever I am.

Redeemed, redeemed,
Redeemed by the blood of the Lamb;
Redeemed, redeemed,
His child and forever I am.

Redeemed, and so happy in Jesus,
No language my rapture can tell;
I know that the light of His presence
With me doth continually dwell.

I think of my blessed Redeemer,
I think of Him all the day long:
I sing, for I cannot be silent;
His love is the theme of my song.

I know there's a crown that is waiting,
In yonder bright mansion for me,
And soon, with the spirits made perfect,
At home with the Lord I shall be.

Read **Psalm 33:1-4.** When you think about Jesus Christ dying on the

…………

cross for your sins, do you sing a song of redemption?

_____
_____
_____
_____
_____
_____

When sharing the gospel, what key words do you need to include in order to share the whole truth?

_____
_____
_____
_____
_____
_____

Read **Ecclesiastes 12:1-7, 13-14.** Do you believe in God, but spend little time with Him in worship?

_____
_____
_____
_____
_____
_____

What are the different ways we offer up worship to God?

_____
_____
_____
_____
_____
_____

PRAYER: It is a privilege to worship You, Lord!

. . . .

WEDNESDAY: WAIT

After WAKING UP, WORSHIPPING, it's time to WAIT upon the Lord…

"But those who WAIT on the LORD shall renew their strength; they shall mount up with wings like eagles, they shall run and not be weary, they shall walk and not faint." **Isaiah 40:31 NKJV**

READ: **Psalm 48:1-1-3, 9-14**
Pray for your:

Family:

_____
_____
_____
_____
_____
_____

Friends:

_____
_____
_____
_____
_____
_____

Community Group:

_____
_____
_____
_____
_____
_____

…………

REVELATION
the End

Church:

_____

_____

_____

_____

_____

_____

Nation:

_____

_____

_____

_____

_____

_____

Leaders:

_____

_____

_____

_____

_____

_____

Yourself:

_____

_____

_____

_____

_____

_____

. . . .

THURSDAY: WORK

After WAKING UP, WORSHIPPING the Lord, and WAITING upon the Lord it's time to WORK...

"WORK hard so God can approve you. Be a good worker, one who does not need to be ashamed and who correctly explains the word of truth." **2 Timothy 2:15 NLT**

The Impact of the Pure
Read: **Revelation 14**

The 144,000 evangelists, are redeemed Jews who receive Jesus Christ as their Lord and Savior during the Tribulation. They are pure, spiritually undefiled saints who choose to resist all of the crazy immoral temptations rampant throughout the world—**Revelation 14:4**. They are blameless, with no deceit found in their mouth—**Revelation 14:5**. And their impact during the Tribulation is great as they reach many in the name of Jesus. Lives are saved. People meet Jesus. God is glorified!

See, there are benefits to living a pure life. If you choose to not play with the world's temptations, you will be able to speak with authority with a witness that matches God's Word. Your voice will impact others for Jesus because people will know that you speak with integrity. However, if you choose to live immorally your voice loses all credibility; as people see you don't practice what you preach. Christian, do you want to be a tool that God can use to reach the lost—**2 Timothy 2:21**? Then choose today to walk in purity, fleeing immorality—**2 Timothy 2:22**.

John tells us that the seal on the foreheads of these 144,000 is God's name—**Revelation 14:1**. God is on the minds of the pure! And they follow Jesus wherever He goes, simply wanting to be in His presence—**Revelation 14:4, Psalm 16:11**. They are loyal to Him no matter the cost—**Luke 9:23**. And they sing a song of redemption that

....

no other can sing — **Revelation 14:3**. Plain and simple, these Christians speak truth and their lives are above approach!

Next, John shares that he sees an angel flying through the heavens proclaiming the gospel. Everyone on earth will have a chance to hear about Jesus! God in His grace and mercy, loves the world so much that up until the last minute He gives people an opportunity to turn from their sin and turn to Him.

But judgment is coming. A second angel comes and says that the government has fallen — **Revelation 14:8**. A third angel follows, shouting to all the unsaved and to those who took the mark of the beast that their fate is sealed for eternity – eternal punishment in hell — **Revelation 14:9-11**. They choose to reject God's love and offer of forgiveness of sins. Christian, there will come a moment in time when Jesus will judge the earth — **Revelation 14:14-20**. Do you know someone who does not know Jesus?

Read **2 Corinthians 5:9-11, Proverbs 23:17,** and **Proverbs 29:25.** What does it mean to "fear God"?

_____
_____
_____
_____
_____
_____

Jesus spoke more about hell than heaven. What did he say? Read **Revelation 14:9-11, Matthew 10:28,** and **Luke 16:19-31.**

_____
_____
_____
_____
_____
_____

Read **Revelation 14:12-13, James 5:10-11, 1 Peter 1:6-7,** and **Mark 13:13.** What does God say about enduring persecution patiently?

_____
_____

_____

_____

_____

_____

Read **Psalm 116:15** and **John 21:18-19.** How does God view the death of His children?

_____

_____

_____

_____

_____

_____

Read **Isaiah 63:1-4.** How does God illustrate His judgment of the wicked?

_____

_____

_____

_____

_____

_____

PRAYER: Lord, thank You for drawing me into Your presence!

. . . .

FRIDAY: WITNESS

After WAKING UP, WORSHIPPING the Lord, WAITING upon the Lord, and WORKING, it's time to WITNESS!

> "But you shall receive power when the Holy Spirit has come upon you; and you shall be WITNESSES to Me...to the end of the earth."
> **Acts 1:8 NKJV**

Read **Revelation 14:3-5, Hebrews 13:4,** and **1 Thessalonians 4:3-8.** Have you made a commitment to remain pure before the Lord?

_____

_____

_____

_____

_____

_____

Read **Revelation 14:1, Colossians 3:2-4,** and **Philippians 4:8.** God is on the mind of those who are pure. Does God occupy your thoughts? Explain.

_____

_____

_____

_____

_____

_____

Read **Ephesians 4:17-32,** and **Romans 12:1-2.** Are you conforming to the world because you fear man or are you fearlessly transforming the world? Explain.

_____

_____

_____

_____

_____

_____

. . . .

Read Revelation 14:12-13, Luke 9:23-24, and **Mark 10:21.** Would you abandon your faith if persecuted, or would you remain loyal to Jesus no matter the cost?

_____

_____

_____

_____

_____

_____

Read 2 Thessalonians 1:4-10 and **2 Timothy 4:6-8.** What does "faithfulness" look like?

_____

_____

_____

_____

_____

_____

Are you being faithful to what God has called you to do?

_____

_____

_____

_____

_____

_____

Read Psalm 139:23-24. Can you enjoy being in the presence of God if there is sin in your life?

_____

_____

_____

_____

_____

Read Luke 10:2. How is your community group going to share the gospel with the lost this week?

_____

....

REVELATION
the End

_____

_____

_____

_____

_____

PRAYER: Lord, please help me to remain faithful to You and the calling You have placed on my life.

. . . .

Week 22: **Revelation 15**

. . . .

MONDAY: WAKE UP

"WAKE UP, for the coming of our salvation is nearer now than when we first believed." **Romans 13:11 NLT**

Lord, please open my eyes to Your heart. Illuminate Your truths to me.

Speak Lord, Your servant listens.

Read: **Revelation 15**

What does the verse say?

_____
_____
_____
_____
_____
_____

What is the lesson?

_____
_____
_____
_____
_____
_____

What is God telling you?

_____
_____
_____
_____
_____

. . . .

What is your commitment?

_____

_____

_____

_____

_____

_____

_____

. . . .

TUESDAY: WORSHIP

After WAKING UP, it's time to WORSHIP...

"But the hour is coming, and is now here, when the true worshippers will WORSHIP the Father in spirit and truth, for the Father is seeking such people to worship him." **John 4:23 ESV**

Joyful Joyful
Henry VanDyke, 1907

Joyful, joyful, we adore Thee
God of glory, Lord of love!
Hearts unfold like flowers before Thee,
Opening to the sun above.
Melt the clouds of sin and sadness;
Drive the dark of doubt away;
Giver of immortal gladness,
Fill us with the light of day!

All Thy works with joy surround Thee,
Earth and heaven reflect Thy rays,
Stars and angels sing around Thee,
Center of unbroken praise.
Field and forest, vale and mountain,
Flowery meadow, flashing sea,
Chanting bird, and flowing fountain
Call us to rejoice in Thee.

Thou art giving and forgiving,
Ever blessing, ever blest,
Well-spring of the joy of living,
Ocean depth of happy rest!
Thou our Father, Christ our Brother—
All who live in love are thine;
Teach us how to love each other,
Lift us to thy joy divine.
Mortals, join the happy chorus,

....

Which the morning stars began;
Love divine is reigning o'er us,
Joining all within its span.
Ever singing, march we onward,
Victors in the midst of strife,
Joyful music leads us Sunward
In the triumph song of life.

Read **Psalm 100.** How would you describe true worship? What is "wrong worship"?

_____

_____

_____

_____

_____

_____

Read **Luke 4:8**. What does the Bible say about worship?

_____

_____

_____

_____

_____

_____

Do your favorite songs focus on praising God for His character and what He has done? Do they focus on the gospel? Or do they focus on self? Do they focus on elevating a worldly mentality?

_____

_____

_____

_____

_____

_____

PRAYER: Thank You, Abba, for giving us the "triumph song of life" in Jesus Christ.

. . . .

WEDNESDAY: WAIT

After WAKING UP, WORSHIPPING, it's time to WAIT upon the Lord…

"But those who WAIT on the LORD shall renew their strength; they shall mount up with wings like eagles, they shall run and not be weary, they shall walk and not faint." **Isaiah 40:31 NKJV**

READ: **Isaiah 61:10-11**
Pray for your:

Family:

_____
_____
_____
_____
_____
_____

Friends:

_____
_____
_____
_____
_____
_____

Community Group:

_____
_____
_____
_____
_____
_____

. . . .

REVELATION
the End

Church:

_____

_____

_____

_____

_____

_____

Nation:

_____

_____

_____

_____

_____

_____

Leaders:

_____

_____

_____

_____

_____

_____

Yourself:

_____

_____

_____

_____

_____

_____

. . . .

THURSDAY: WORK

After WAKING UP, WORSHIPPING the Lord, and WAITING upon the Lord it's time to WORK...

"WORK hard so God can approve you. Be a good worker, one who does not need to be ashamed and who correctly explains the word of truth." **2 Timothy 2:15 NLT**

Victory!
Read: **Revelation 15**

Christian! Have you ever heard God say to your heart, "I have planned this so I will receive great glory at the expense of Satan" — **Exodus 14:4**? Life here on earth and life in heaven is all about God's glory! It's not about you — it's about God. So the crazy trials he allows you to go through are so that He receives the glory, as the world watches Him miraculously deliver you. When you are weak, He is strong. Rest assured, His grace is sufficient for you — **2 Corinthians 12:9**.

Here in **Revelation 15,** we see in heaven, God receiving glory as His people sing a song of deliverance, praising Him for His victory over the Antichrist. Though they suffered greatly at the hands of Antichrist, not one word of complaint comes from their mouth, or a word on how they sacrificed much for Christ. Their humble worship, the song of Moses and the song of the Lamb, glorifies God, extolling His character — **Revelation 15:3-4**.

In the book of **Revelation** we see God's holiness displayed in His divine wrath. Holiness demands the judgment of sin. So, we see His wrath continuously poured out on sinful mankind, calling people to repentance. Each judgment increases with intensity, beginning with the seven seal judgments opened in **Revelation 6.** Then the seventh seal judgment released the seven trumpet judgments — **Revelation 8:1-9:21**, and the seventh trumpet judgment released the seven bowl judgments — **Revelation 11:15; 16:1-21**. This wrath is not an impulsive

....

outburst of anger on God's part; it is a calculated, measured response to sin. God hates sin! Here in **Revelation 15,** we see God introduce the seven bowl judgments, the most severe judgments God will ever pour out.

Read **2 Corinthians 4:16-18.** How does God encourage believers?

_____
_____
_____
_____
_____
_____

Read **Exodus 15:1-18.** What is Israel doing? Describe the Song of Moses.

_____
_____
_____
_____
_____
_____

Write out **John 17:24.**

_____
_____
_____
_____
_____
_____

The seven gold bowls are filled with the terrible wrath of God — **Revelation 15:7**. What does the Bible say about God's wrath? **1 Thessalonians 5:9, Ephesians 5:6, Romans 5:9, Romans 1:18-21.**

_____
_____
_____
_____
_____
_____

. . . .

PRAYER: Father, thank You for sending Your Son to die on the cross for me, taking the wrath I deserved upon Himself.

....

FRIDAY: WITNESS

After WAKING UP, WORSHIPPING the Lord, WAITING upon the Lord, and WORKING, it's time to WITNESS!

"But you shall receive power when the Holy Spirit has come upon you; and you shall be WITNESSES to Me...to the end of the earth."
Acts 1:8 NKJV

Describe a time when God delivered you from a trial.

_____
_____
_____
_____
_____
_____

Read **Romans 8:28-29.** What did you learn from that trial? Share a verse.

_____
_____
_____
_____
_____
_____

Read **2 Corinthians 12:9-10.** In your trial, what did you learn about God's grace?

_____
_____
_____
_____
_____
_____

Read **Psalm 103:1-8.** When you think back to your trial, do you complain about what you had to go through or do you focus on glorifying God and His character? Explain.

. . . .

_____
_____
_____
_____
_____
_____
_____

Read **Colossians 3:1-4.** How are you focusing on heaven?

_____
_____
_____
_____
_____
_____

Read **Revelation 15:2** and **1 Corinthians 10:13.** Describe a time when you were victorious over the temptation to do evil.

_____
_____
_____
_____
_____
_____

Read **Romans 3:23, 6:23, 10:9-10.** Do you know someone who will experience God's wrath unless they receive Jesus Christ as their Lord and Savior? What are you going to do?

_____
_____
_____
_____
_____
_____

PRAYER: Abba! Who do You want me to share Jesus Christ with?

. . . .

REVELATION
the End

. . . .

Week 23: **Revelation 16**

· ·

MONDAY: WAKE UP

"WAKE UP, for the coming of our salvation is nearer now than when we first believed." **Romans 13:11 NLT**

Lord, please open my eyes to Your heart. Illuminate Your truths to me.
Speak Lord, Your servant listens.

Read: **Revelation 16**

What does the verse say?

_____
_____
_____
_____
_____
_____

What is the lesson?

_____
_____
_____
_____
_____
_____

What is God telling you?

_____
_____
_____
_____
_____

· · · · · · · · · · ·

REVELATION
the End

What is your commitment?

_____

_____

_____

_____

_____

_____

_____

. . . .

TUESDAY: WORSHIP

After WAKING UP, it's time to WORSHIP...

"But the hour is coming, and is now here, when the true worshippers will WORSHIP the Father in spirit and truth, for the Father is seeking such people to worship him." **John 4:23 ESV**

In Evil Long I Took Delight
John Newton 1779

In evil long I took delight
Unawed by shame or fear;
Till a new object struck my sight
And stopped my wild career.
I saw one hanging on a tree
In agonies and blood;
Who fixed his languid eyes on me
As near his cross I stood.
Sure never till my latest breath
Can I forget that look;
It seemed to charge me with his death
Though not a word he spoke.
My conscience felt and owned the guilt
And plunged me in despair;
I saw my sins his blood had spilt
And helped to nail him there.
Alas, I knew not what I did
But now my tears are vain;
Where shall my trembling soul be hid?
For I the Lord have slain.
A second look he gave which said
"I freely all forgive;
This blood is for thy ransom paid
I died that thou mayest live."

Thus while his death my sin displays
In all its blackest hue;

....

Such is the mystery of grace,
It seals my pardon too.
With pleasing grief and mournful joy
My spirit now is filled;
That I should such a life destroy
Yet live by him I killed.

When you think about Jesus Christ on the cross dying for your sins, what comes to mind?

_____

_____

_____

_____

_____

_____

Read **Ephesians 2:8-9.** Describe God's grace.

_____

_____

_____

_____

_____

Read **Revelation 16:15.** Why does worship keep people awake, ready for Christ's return?

_____

_____

_____

_____

_____

_____

PRAYER: Please give me the eyes to see and the ears to hear; those are the gifts I want, as I wait for Christ's return.

. . . .

WEDNESDAY: WAIT

After WAKING UP, WORSHIPPING, it's time to WAIT upon the Lord…

"But those who WAIT on the LORD shall renew their strength; they shall mount up with wings like eagles, they shall run and not be weary, they shall walk and not faint." **Isaiah 40:31 NKJV**

READ: **Romans 13:11-14**
Pray for your:

Family:

_____
_____
_____
_____
_____
_____

Friends:

_____
_____
_____
_____
_____
_____

Community Group:

_____
_____
_____
_____
_____
_____

. . . .

REVELATION
the End

Church:

_____
_____
_____
_____
_____
_____
_____

Nation:

_____
_____
_____
_____
_____
_____
_____

Leaders:

_____
_____
_____
_____
_____
_____
_____

Yourself:

_____
_____
_____
_____
_____
_____
_____

. . . .

THURSDAY: WORK

After WAKING UP, WORSHIPPING the Lord, and WAITING upon the Lord it's time to WORK...

"WORK hard so God can approve you. Be a good worker, one who does not need to be ashamed and who correctly explains the word of truth." **2 Timothy 2:15 NLT**

Stay Awake!
Read: **Revelation 16**

God disciplines and punishes people in the perfect way to get their attention—**Revelation 16:7, Hebrews 10:26-31**. Here in **Revelation 16,** we see God's wrath poured out on sinful mankind, in the seven bowl judgments. Yet, the people still refuse to repent because their hearts are hard. They will spend eternity in hell, a place void of God's presence and glory—**2 Thessalonians 1:9**.

Christian! People do not have to experience this wrath. God in His love, knew we would need a Savior to save us from the repercussions of our sin. So, He sent His one and only Son, Jesus Christ, to walk this earth, living a perfect life, dying a horrific death for us on the cross—**2 Corinthians 5:21**. Jesus bore the wrath we deserved on the cross. His shed blood, covered our sins past, present, and future—**Hebrews 9:22**. He was buried in a tomb, but He didn't stay dead! He rose again on the third day—**1 Corinthians 15:3**-4, and He is now sitting at God's right hand—**Hebrews 1:3**. Jesus is alive! He stood in the gap for you, providing a way for you to stand justified in God's sight, just as if you never sinned. Christian have you been playing with sin, thinking you could get away with it? Did you get caught? Does it matter? Do you need to repent and rededicate your life to Jesus Christ?

Amidst the details of the seven bowl judgments God gives a word of encouragement to the Christian—"stay awake"—**Revelation 16:5**. Jesus Christ is coming back soon, so the sleeping church needs to wake up—**Ephesians 5:14**; and the Christian who "woke up" needs to

....

not fall back asleep but to "stay awake." How? Community. When we gather together in fellowship, discipleship and mission our hearts are united with a love for Jesus and furthering His Kingdom here on earth. When one heart's on fire, it ignites another. So, do not neglect meeting together, as some people do, but encourage and warn each other, especially now that the day of his coming again is drawing near — **Hebrews 10:25**.

List the seven bowl judgments:

1. _____
2. _____
3. _____
4. _____
5. _____
6. _____
7. _____

Read **Hebrews 3:12-15.** What does the Bible say about "hardened hearts"?

_____
_____
_____
_____
_____
_____

Read **Matthew 25:30, Luke 16:24-26,** and **2 Thessalonians 1:8-9.** How does the Bible describe hell?

_____
_____
_____
_____
_____
_____

In the midst of war and slaughter, God gives a word of encouragement and hope to the believers. Read **Revelation 16:15.** What does He say?

. . . .

_____

_____

_____

_____

_____

_____

PRAYER: Father, please place people in my path so that I can share Jesus Christ with them.

FRIDAY: WITNESS

After WAKING UP, WORSHIPPING the Lord, WAITING upon the Lord, and WORKING, it's time to WITNESS!

"But you shall receive power when the Holy Spirit has come upon you; and you shall be WITNESSES to Me...to the end of the earth."
Acts 1:8 NKJV

Read **1 Thessalonians 5:10-11, 14-15.** How are the people in your community group living out these truths?

_____

_____

_____

_____

_____

_____

How is your community group going to "stay awake" — **Revelation 16:15**?

_____

_____

_____

_____

_____

_____

Who are you going to share the gospel with this week?

_____

_____

_____

_____

_____

_____

Read **John 14:6.** Pray for God to open people's eyes to His truth.

_____

. . . .

_____
_____
_____
_____
_____

If your friend wants to receive Jesus Christ into their life as their Lord and Savior, all they have to do is:

1. Realize that they are a sinner. Romans 3:23
2. Recognize that Jesus died on the cross for them. Romans 5:8
3. Repent of their sin. Acts 3:19
4. Receive Christ into their life. Romans 10:9

And they can pray a prayer like this one:

Dear Lord Jesus, I know that I am a sinner. I believe You died on the cross for my sins and that you rose again from the dead. I repent of my sins. I confess You as my personal Lord and Savior. Please help me to follow You every day of my life. Thank you for saving me. In Jesus' name, Amen.

Describe the most memorable time in your community group that got your heart on fire to serve Jesus, furthering His Kingdom.

_____
_____
_____
_____
_____
_____

Write your prayer:

_____
_____
_____
_____
_____
_____

. . . .

REVELATION
the End

. . . .

Week 24: Revelation 17-18

....

MONDAY: WAKE UP

"WAKE UP, for the coming of our salvation is nearer now than when we first believed." **Romans 13:11 NLT**

Lord, please open my eyes to Your heart. Illuminate Your truths to me. Speak Lord, Your servant listens.

Read: **Revelation 17-18**

What does the verse say?

_____

_____

_____

_____

_____

_____

What is the lesson?

_____

_____

_____

_____

_____

_____

What is God telling you?

_____

_____

_____

_____

_____

....

What is your commitment?

_____
_____
_____
_____
_____
_____
_____

TUESDAY: WORSHIP

After WAKING UP, it's time to WORSHIP...

"But the hour is coming, and is now here, when the true worshippers will WORSHIP the Father in spirit and truth, for the Father is seeking such people to worship him." **John 4:23 ESV**

A Mighty Fortress Is Our God
Martin Luther, 1529

A mighty fortress is our God,
A bulwark never failing;
Our helper He, amid the flood
Of mortal ills prevailing;
For still our ancient foe
Doth seek to work us woe;
His craft and power are great,
And armed with cruel hate,
On earth is not his equal.

Did we in our strength confide,
Our striving would be losing;
Were not the right Man on our side,
The Man of God's own choosing;
Dost ask who that may be?
Christ Jesus, it is He;
Lord Sabaoth, His name,
From age to age the same.
And He must win the battle.

And though this world, with devils filled,
Should threaten to undo us,
We will not fear, for God hath willed
His truth to triumph through us;
The prince of darkness grim,
We tremble not for him;
His rage we can endure,

. . . .

For lo, his doom is sure;
One little word shall fell him.

That word above all earthly powers,
No thanks to them, abideth;
The Spirit and the gifts are ours
Through Him who with us sideth.
Let goods and kindred go,
This mortal life also;
The body they may kill;
God's truth abideth still:
His kingdom is forever.

Read **Revelation 18:8** and **Psalm 27:1**. Why do we have nothing to fear?

_____
_____
_____
_____
_____
_____

Read **John 14:14**. What word stops Satan? Why?

_____
_____
_____
_____
_____
_____

Does your knowledge of God affect your worship of Him? Explain.

_____
_____
_____
_____
_____
_____

. . . .

Does your passion in worship vary due to what you are going through? Why or why not?

_____

_____

_____

_____

_____

_____

In the past couple of weeks, has your heart been truly surrendered to God in worship? Why or why not?

_____

_____

_____

_____

_____

_____

What impacts your heart and mind the most during worship – the music, the lyrics, or both? Explain.

_____

_____

_____

_____

_____

_____

PRAYER: Abba! Thank You for remaining the same and never changing. My heart belongs to You.

....

WEDNESDAY: WAIT

After WAKING UP, WORSHIPPING, it's time to WAIT upon the Lord…

"But those who WAIT on the LORD shall renew their strength; they shall mount up with wings like eagles, they shall run and not be weary, they shall walk and not faint." **Isaiah 40:31 NKJV**

READ: **Mathew 6:9-13**
Pray for your:

Family:

_____

_____

_____

_____

_____

_____

Friends:

_____

_____

_____

_____

_____

_____

Community Group:

_____

_____

_____

_____

_____

_____

…………

WEEK TWENTY-FOUR

Church:

_____
_____
_____
_____
_____
_____
_____

Nation:

_____
_____
_____
_____
_____
_____
_____

Leaders:

_____
_____
_____
_____
_____
_____
_____

Yourself:

_____
_____
_____
_____
_____
_____
_____

. . . .

THURSDAY: WORK

After WAKING UP, WORSHIPPING the Lord, and WAITING upon the Lord it's time to WORK...

"WORK hard so God can approve you. Be a good worker, one who does not need to be ashamed and who correctly explains the word of truth." **2 Timothy 2:15 NLT**

Everything Can Change in a Minute!
Read: **Revelation 17 & 18**

"Sin, when it is full-grown, brings forth death" — **James 1:15 NKJV**. So don't play with it! Here in **Revelation 17,** we see prosperous Babylon openly mocking God, worshipping idols, and then soon in **Revelation 18,** we see their destruction. God is Sovereign and will not be mocked — **Galatians 6:7**. Everything can change in a minute — **Revelation 18:17**. People will reap what they sow — **Galatians 6:7**, so listen when God says: You shall have no other gods before Me, you shall not make for yourself a carved image, and you shall not take the Lord's name in vain — **Exodus 20:3-7**.

The harlot — **Revelation 17:1** represents Babylon, a powerful world system of false religion. The non-believers are intoxicated with her — **Revelation 17:2**, idolizing her and the false religious system. She is seen sitting on a scarlet beast, which is the Antichrist — **Revelation 17:3**. Now Antichrist supports the harlot and the false religious system for a time, to promote unity amongst the people, but then he overthrows it and takes control — **Revelation 17:16**. Antichrist wants all of the power and the worship for himself. But this is all a part of God's plan — **Revelation 17:17**.

We also see the ten-nation confederacy and the Antichrist try to make war with the Lamb, Jesus Christ, referencing Armageddon — **Revelation 17:14**. A futile effort as the Lamb destroys the kings — **Revelation 19:17-21**. Jesus Christ is Sovereign and in control over all rulers, not one attempt to fight Him will win — **Revelation 19:16**.

....

In **Revelation 18,** we see God destroy Babylon. There is a specific time when God will judge the wicked and avenge the blood of the apostles and prophets who were killed — **Revelation 18:20**. God promised He would — **Revelation 6:10-11**, and He keeps His promises. God's righteousness and justice always prevails.

Read **Revelation 18.** Describe the details of Babylon's destruction.

_____

_____

_____

_____

_____

_____

Read **Genesis 19:1-29.** What happened when God called Lot and his family to separate themselves from the evil found in Sodom and Gomorrah?

_____

_____

_____

_____

_____

_____

Read **Matthew 10:28.** What does Jesus say?

_____

_____

_____

_____

_____

_____

Read **James 4:4-10.** What warning does the Bible give to those who are "friends with the world"?

_____

_____

_____

_____

_____

. . . .

Read **2 Timothy 3:16-17.** What will keep Christians from falling away from the Lord, and living in habitual sin?

_____
_____
_____
_____
_____
_____
_____

PRAYER: Father, thank You for Your Truth!

. . . .

FRIDAY: WITNESS

After WAKING UP, WORSHIPPING the Lord, WAITING upon the Lord, and WORKING, it's time to WITNESS!

"But you shall receive power when the Holy Spirit has come upon you; and you shall be WITNESSES to Me...to the end of the earth."
Acts 1:8 NKJV

Read **Jeremiah 3:6-9.** The people in Babylon idolized Antichrist and his religious world system—**Revelation 17.** Have you ever idolized something/someone?

_____

_____

_____

_____

_____

_____

What were the repercussions? Share a verse.

_____

_____

_____

_____

_____

Read **1 John 5:21 and Galatians 6:1-3.** How are you going to hold the people in your community group accountable, so they do not sin by idolizing?

_____

_____

_____

_____

_____

_____

....

Read **Revelation 18:4.** Do you need to separate yourself from the evil influences around you? Explain.

_____
_____
_____
_____
_____
_____

List the type of evil influences you and your friends face every day.

_____
_____
_____
_____
_____
_____

Read **2 Corinthians 6:14-7:1.** How are you going to live out these verses?

_____
_____
_____
_____
_____
_____

Read **Hebrews 12:12-13.** Who is following you? Will they stumble if they do what you are currently doing?

_____
_____
_____
_____
_____
_____

Read **2 Peter 3:9-10.** How is your community group witnessing to non-believers?

_____
_____
_____

Write your prayer:

REVELATION
the End

. . . .

Week 25: Revelation 19

. . . .

MONDAY: WAKE UP

"WAKE UP, for the coming of our salvation is nearer now than when we first believed." **Romans 13:11 NLT**

Lord, please open my eyes to Your heart. Illuminate Your truths to me. Speak Lord, Your servant listens.

Read: **Revelation 19**

What does the verse say?

_____
_____
_____
_____
_____
_____

What is the lesson?

_____
_____
_____
_____
_____
_____

What is God telling you?

_____
_____
_____
_____
_____
_____

. . . .

What is your commitment?

_____

_____

_____

_____

_____

_____

_____

. . . .

TUESDAY: WORSHIP

After WAKING UP, it's time to WORSHIP…

"But the hour is coming, and is now here, when the true worshippers will WORSHIP the Father in spirit and truth, for the Father is seeking such people to worship him." **John 4:23 ESV**

Mine Eyes Have Seen the Glory
Julia Ward Howe, 1862

Mine eyes have seen the glory of the coming of the Lord;
He is trampling out the vintage where the grapes of wrath are stored;
He hath loosed the fateful lightning of His terrible, swift sword;
His truth is marching on.

Chorus:
Glory! Glory, hallelujah!
Glory! Glory, hallelujah!
Glory! Glory, hallelujah!
Our God is marching on!

I have seen Him in the watchfires of a hundred circling camps;
They have builded Him an altar in the evening dews and damps;
I can read His righteous sentence by the dim and flaring lamps;
His day is marching on. [Chorus]

He has sounded forth the trumpet that shall never sound retreat;
He is sifting out the hearts of men before His judgment seat;
O be swift, my soul, to answer Him; be jubilant my feet!
Our God is marching on. [Chorus]

In the beauty of the lilies Christ was born across the sea,
With a glory in His bosom that transfigures you and me;
As He died to make men holy, let us live to make men free,
While God is marching on. [Chorus]

He is coming like the glory of the morning on the wave;

…………

He is wisdom to the mighty, He is honor to the brave;
So the world shall be His footstool, and the soul of wrong His slave.
Our God is marching on. [Chorus]

Read **Revelation 4:8, 11; 5:9-14; 7:11-12; 11:16-18.** Describe the
worship and praise of God in heaven.

_____
_____
_____
_____
_____
_____

What are you doing, when no one is watching?

_____
_____
_____
_____
_____
_____

Is your heart right before God? If not, how are you going to make it
right? Share a verse.

_____
_____
_____
_____
_____
_____

Write your prayer:

_____
_____
_____
_____
_____
_____

. . . .

WEDNESDAY: WAIT

After WAKING UP, WORSHIPPING, it's time to WAIT upon the Lord…

"But those who WAIT on the LORD shall renew their strength; they shall mount up with wings like eagles, they shall run and not be weary, they shall walk and not faint." **Isaiah 40:31 NKJV**

READ: **Philippians 1:9-11, 1 Corinthians 15:58, Philippians 2:14-16**
Pray for your:

Family:

_____
_____
_____
_____
_____
_____

Friends:

_____
_____
_____
_____
_____
_____

Community Group:

_____
_____
_____
_____
_____
_____

. . . .

REVELATION
the End

Church:

_____
_____
_____
_____
_____
_____
_____

Nation:

_____
_____
_____
_____
_____
_____

Leaders:

_____
_____
_____
_____
_____
_____

Yourself:

_____
_____
_____
_____
_____
_____

. . . .

THURSDAY: WORK

After WAKING UP, WORSHIPPING the Lord, and WAITING upon the Lord it's time to WORK...

"WORK hard so God can approve you. Be a good worker, one who does not need to be ashamed and who correctly explains the word of truth." **2 Timothy 2:15 NLT**

Praising Jesus Is Contagious!
Read **Revelation 19**

Praising Jesus is contagious! You can't help but smile and praise God when you are around people who are bubbling over with excitement over how good God is. It's contagious! When you see God answer your friend's prayer, when you witness God delivering a family member from a drawn out trial, when your own faith is made sight, the words "Praise the Lord" immediately escape from your mouth and you can't help but smile. That's what is happening here in heaven. John sees a vast crowd praising God. God is eternally faithful; when we are faithless, He is faithful still—**2 Timothy 2:13**.

Here John witnesses God delivering His people—**Revelation 19:1**, judging the sinner, avenging His people's blood—**Revelation 19:2**, stopping man's rebellion—**Revelation 19:3**, reigning in Sovereignty—**Revelation 19:6**, and communing with His people at the ultimate marriage feast—**Revelation 19:7**. The people in heaven can't help but praise Him—the end of rebellion is at hand. Our God saves!

Christian, God's timing is perfect. Wait. Be patient. For at the right time our Bridegroom will come for us, the church, and we will sit with Him at the ultimate wedding celebration—**Revelation 19:7, Ephesians 1:4**, with the Old Testament saints and the Tribulation saints as our guests—**Revelation 19:9**. But in the meantime we must prepare, for our wedding garments will be made up of the good deeds we do on earth—**Revelation 19:8**. So today, Christian, where is your focus? Where is your heart? Are you consumed with menial

....

worldly issues that distract you or are you concentrating on living out
God's purpose for your life?

**Read Revelation 19:1, Isaiah 12:2, Ephesians 3:12, Hebrews 2:14-15,
Hebrews 10:22, 1 John 5:13.** What is salvation? (Ask a different
question on salvation)

_____
_____
_____
_____
_____
_____

Read **Revelation 19:1-7.** Why are the people in heaven praising God?

_____
_____
_____
_____
_____
_____

Read **Revelation 19:11.** Explain why Jesus' name is "Faithful and
True." Share verses.

_____
_____
_____
_____
_____
_____

Describe the difference between the Rapture and the Second Coming
of Jesus Christ:

RAPTURE: Read **1 Corinthians 15:51-54, 1 Thessalonians 4:13-18,
John 14:1-4, Revelation 3:10-11.**

_____
_____
_____

. . . .

_____
_____
_____

SECOND COMING: Read **Matthew 24:29-30, Revelation 1:7, Revelation 19:11-21.**

_____
_____
_____
_____
_____
_____

Read Revelation 19:13. How powerful is the Word of God? Share a verse.

_____
_____
_____
_____
_____
_____

Read **Revelation 19:15-21** (see also: **Psalm 2:1-9, Isaiah 66:15-16,** and **2 Thessalonians 1:7-9**). Describe the Battle of Armageddon.

_____
_____
_____
_____
_____
_____

PRAYER: Jesus! You are the only One worthy of praise and honor. Thank you for dying on the cross for my sins, giving me the hope of eternal life in heaven with You!

. . . .

FRIDAY: WITNESS

After WAKING UP, WORSHIPPING the Lord, WAITING upon the Lord, and WORKING, it's time to WITNESS!

> "But you shall receive power when the Holy Spirit has come upon you; and you shall be WITNESSES to Me...to the end of the earth."
> **Acts 1:8 NKJV**

Read **Revelation 19:1.** What characteristics are found in people who are truly saved? What is the evidence of their salvation? Read **Revelation 17:14, Romans 16:19, Matthew 5:8, Colossians 1:4,** and **John 10:4.**

_____
_____
_____
_____
_____
_____

Are those characteristics found in you?

_____
_____
_____
_____
_____

What areas do you need to grow in? Share a verse.

_____
_____
_____
_____
_____

Read **Revelation 19:2** and **Romans 12:19.** Have you ever witnessed God correct someone who was in the wrong and/or rescue someone

. . . .

who was being unjustly persecuted?

_____
_____
_____
_____
_____
_____

How does this encourage you and warn you at the same time?

_____
_____
_____
_____
_____
_____

Read **Revelation 19:7** and **1 Corinthians 10:31.** Today, how can you "honor" God or "give God glory"?

_____
_____
_____
_____
_____
_____

Read **Revelation 19:10.** When you talk to people, do you "give a clear witness for Jesus"? What does that look like?

_____
_____
_____
_____
_____
_____

Revelation 19:10b NLT "For the essence of prophecy is to give a clear witness for Jesus." Read **Proverbs 20:12.** Today, pray for the Lord to open your eyes to the opportunities He gives to you and your community group to share the gospel and minister to the lost. Share what happened.

. . . .

_____
_____
_____
_____
_____
_____
_____

How has the Word of God impacted your life? Share a verse.

_____
_____
_____
_____
_____
_____

How is your community group going to encourage people to read their Bibles?

_____
_____
_____
_____
_____
_____

Write your prayer:

_____
_____
_____
_____
_____
_____

. . . .

Week 26: **Revelation 20**

. . . .

MONDAY: WAKE UP

"WAKE UP, for the coming of our salvation is nearer now than when we first believed." **Romans 13:11 NLT**

Lord, please open my eyes to Your heart. Illuminate Your truths to me.

Speak Lord, Your servant listens.

Read: **Revelation 20**

What does the verse say?

_____
_____
_____
_____
_____
_____

What is the lesson?

_____
_____
_____
_____
_____
_____

What is God telling you?

_____
_____
_____
_____

. . . .

_____

_____

What is your commitment?

_____

_____

_____

_____

_____

_____

. . . .

TUESDAY: WORSHIP

After WAKING UP, it's time to WORSHIP...

"But the hour is coming, and is now here, when the true worshippers will WORSHIP the Father in spirit and truth, for the Father is seeking such people to worship him." **John 4:23 ESV**

The Church's One Foundation
S.J. Stone, 1866

The church's one foundation
Is Jesus Christ, her Lord;
She is his new creation
By water and the Word:
From heav'n he came and sought her
To be his holy bride;
With his own blood he bought her,
And for her life he died.

Elect from ev'ry nation,
Yet one o'er all the earth,
Her charter of salvation
One Lord, one faith, one birth;
One holy name she blesses,
Partakes one holy food,
And to one hope she presses,
With ev'ry grace endued.

Though with a scornful wonder
Men see her sore oppressed,
By schisms rent asunder,
By heresies distressed,
Yet saints their watch are keeping,
Their cry goes up, "How long?"
And soon the night of weeping
Shall be the morn of song.

....

The church shall never perish!
Her dear Lord to defend,
To guide, sustain, and cherish,
Is with her to the end;
Though there be those that hate her,
And false sons in her pale,
Against both foe and traitor
She ever shall prevail.

'Mid toil and tribulation,
And tumult of her war,
She waits the consummation
Of peace forevermore;
Till with the vision glorious
Her longing eyes are blest,
And the great church victorious
Shall be the church at rest.

Yet she on earth hath union
With the God the Three in One,
And mystic sweet communion
With those whose rest is won:
O happy ones and holy!
Lord, give us grace that we,
Like them, the meek and lowly,
On high may dwell with thee.

Read **Isaiah 45:5-6.** Knowing that there is no other God apart from
God, how are you going to worship and praise Him today?

_____
_____
_____
_____
_____
_____

Read **Jeremiah 31:33-34, 2 Timothy 2:15, Psalm 95:6-7,** and **John 4:23.**
Why do we need a healthy balance of the two: the Word and
Worship?

. . . .

_____

_____

_____

_____

_____

_____

How many worship songs do you have memorized? Do you have the
same amount of Scripture verses memorized? Why?

_____

_____

_____

_____

_____

_____

Read 2 Corinthians 13:5. When analyzing your own walk with the
Lord, would you say you have a strong foundation on Jesus Christ?

_____

_____

_____

_____

_____

_____

Write your prayer:

_____

_____

_____

_____

_____

. . . .

WEDNESDAY: WAIT

After WAKING UP, WORSHIPPING, it's time to WAIT upon the Lord...

> "But those who WAIT on the LORD shall renew their strength; they shall mount up with wings like eagles, they shall run and not be weary, they shall walk and not faint." **Isaiah 40:31 NKJV**

READ: **Jeremiah 17:10**
Pray for your:

Family:

_____
_____
_____
_____
_____

Friends:

_____
_____
_____
_____
_____

Community Group:

_____
_____
_____
_____
_____

W E E K *TWENTY - SIX*

Church:

_____
_____
_____
_____
_____
_____

Nation:

_____
_____
_____
_____
_____
_____

Leaders:

_____
_____
_____
_____
_____
_____

Yourself:

_____
_____
_____
_____
_____
_____

. . . .

THURSDAY: WORK

After WAKING UP, WORSHIPPING the Lord, and WAITING upon the Lord it's time to WORK...

"WORK hard so God can approve you. Be a good worker, one who does not need to be ashamed and who correctly explains the word of truth." **2 Timothy 2:15 NLT**

Jesus Reigns!
Read **Revelation 20**

Christian, Satan is not all-powerful. Only God is! As we read **Revelation 20**, we see that one angel captured Satan easily, binding him with chains for 1,000 years. Satan cannot do anything he wants, he is at the constant mercy of God—**Job 1:12**. So when God says, "Satan, you are done inflicting pain on My people," he's done. Praise God!

So during Jesus Christ's 1,000 year reign on earth there will be peace. Satan is locked up; so there is no sin, turmoil, fear or despair. The Tribulation saints, the Old and New Testament saints and the redeemed will rule and reign with Christ—**Revelation 20:4, 2 Timothy 2:12**. Life is really good. Think perfection. Jesus is with you.

But then, at the end of the 1,000 year reign, Jesus releases Satan for his final chance to deceive. In His love for His people, Christ gives them the opportunity to choose Him or Satan. Jesus never forces Himself upon anyone. The sad thing is, many descendants of the Tribulation saints, who grew up in the 1,000 year reign living in absolute perfection in the presence of Jesus Christ, will walk away from Him choosing the path of destruction. Sometimes we believe that if only the circumstances surrounding us were perfect, it would be easier to believe. But that's not the case; it's a matter of the heart. Today, where is your heart?

There is coming a day when every knee will bow and tongue will

....

confess that Jesus Christ is Lord — **Philippians 2:10-11**. The question is: which judgment will you be standing at? The judgment for Christians, which is more like an awards ceremony, or the Great White Throne Judgment for non-believers?

Today is the day to choose where you are going when you die. Heaven or hell? There is coming a day when God will throw Satan into hell, for good. Christian, hell was not made for people; it was made for Satan and his demons. God does not want you there. Picture Him looking you in the eye saying, "Over my dead body, will you go to hell!" Jesus' dead body! But in His love, as the perfect gentleman, He gives you a choice. To not say yes to Jesus' gift of salvation, is to say no. So, if you do not choose to respond to His sacrificial love, by accepting Him as your Lord and Savior, you are literally stepping over His dead body that was laid down for you – choosing to walk straight into hell. It's your choice.

Read **Revelation 20:3** and **Matthew 4:1-11.** How does Satan try to deceive Christians?

_____
_____
_____
_____
_____
_____

What do the prophets say about the millennial reign of Jesus Christ?

Isaiah 11:6-12:

_____
_____
_____
_____
_____
_____

Micah 4:1-8:

_____
_____

....

_____

_____

_____

_____

(See also: **Zephaniah 3:14-20** and **Matthew 24:29-31, 36-44**)

Read **Revelation 20:11-13** and **Daniel 7:9-10.** What is the Great White Throne Judgment?

_____

_____

_____

_____

_____

_____

Read **1 Corinthians 3:11-15, 2 Corinthians 5:10-11, and Romans 14:10-12.** What is the Judgment seat of Christ?

_____

_____

_____

_____

_____

_____

How does the Judgment seat of Christ differ from the Great White Throne Judgment?

_____

_____

_____

_____

_____

_____

PRAYER: Thank you Jesus for loving me so much that You give me the opportunity to choose You. I choose You today!

. . . .

FRIDAY: WITNESS

After WAKING UP, WORSHIPPING the Lord, WAITING upon the Lord, and WORKING, it's time to WITNESS!

> "But you shall receive power when the Holy Spirit has come upon you; and you shall be WITNESSES to Me...to the end of the earth."
> **Acts 1:8 NKJV**

Share the gospel in one minute. Include verses.

_____
_____
_____
_____
_____
_____

What will it be like to live on earth with Jesus Christ as the ruler? (Example: No more fear.)

_____
_____
_____
_____
_____
_____

Read **2 Peter 3:18.** How are Christians to grow in their knowledge of Jesus?

_____
_____
_____
_____
_____
_____

Read **Philippians 1:20-25** and **1 Corinthians 9:24-27.** Do you care how you live for the Lord?

. . . .

Read **Matthew 5:48** and **1 Peter 1:15-16.** What standard does God hold people to?

Read **Matthew 12:37, Matthew 16:28, Luke 8:17** and **Romans 2:16.** How will God judge non-believers?

Why do Christians have hope? Share a verse.

Today, is your conscience clear? Read **1 John 1:7-9.** What sins do you need to confess?

. . . .

Write your prayer:

_____

_____

_____

_____

_____

_____

. . . .

REVELATION
the End

. . . .

Week 27: Revelation 21

. . . .

MONDAY: WAKE UP

"WAKE UP, for the coming of our salvation is nearer now than when we first believed." **Romans 13:11 NLT**

Lord, please open my eyes to Your heart. Illuminate Your truths to me.

Speak Lord, Your servant listens.

Read: **Revelation 21**

What does the verse say?

_____
_____
_____
_____
_____
_____

What is the lesson?

_____
_____
_____
_____
_____
_____

What is God telling you?

_____
_____
_____
_____
_____
_____

. . . .

REVELATION
the End

What is your commitment?

_____

_____

_____

_____

_____

_____

. . . .

TUESDAY: WORSHIP

After WAKING UP, it's time to WORSHIP…

"But the hour is coming, and is now here, when the true worshippers will WORSHIP the Father in spirit and truth, for the Father is seeking such people to worship him." **John 4:23 ESV**

O Holy City, Seen of John,
Walter Russell Bowie, 1909

O holy city, seen of John,
Where Christ, the Lamb, does reign,
Within whose four-square walls shall come
No night, nor need, nor pain,
And where the tears are wiped from eyes
That shall not weep again!

O shame to us who rest content
While lust and greed for gain
In street and shop and tenement
Wring gold from human pain,
And bitter lips in deep despair
Cry, "Christ has died in vain!"

Give us, O God, the strength to build
The city that has stood
Too long a dream; whose laws are love,
Whose ways are servant-hood,
And where the sun that shines becomes
Your grace for human good.

Already in the mind of God
That city rises fair.
Lo, how its splendor challenges
The souls that greatly dare,

…………

and bids us seize the whole of life
and build its glory there.

Jesus Christ reigns! Write a couple of lines to a worship song about
Christ's ultimate authority over mankind.

_____
_____
_____
_____
_____
_____

Read **Revelation 21:3-4**. How do these verses impact your worship?

_____
_____
_____
_____
_____
_____

Explain this hymn.

_____
_____
_____
_____
_____
_____

Write your prayer:

_____
_____
_____
_____
_____
_____

. . . .

WEDNESDAY: WAIT

After WAKING UP, WORSHIPPING, it's time to WAIT upon the Lord…

"But those who WAIT on the LORD shall renew their strength; they shall mount up with wings like eagles, they shall run and not be weary, they shall walk and not faint." **Isaiah 40:31 NKJV**

READ: **Ecclesiastes 3:11-13**
Pray for your:

Family:

_____
_____
_____
_____
_____
_____

Friends:

_____
_____
_____
_____
_____
_____

Community Group:

_____
_____
_____
_____
_____
_____

…………

REVELATION
the End

Church:

_____
_____
_____
_____
_____
_____
_____

Nation:

_____
_____
_____
_____
_____
_____
_____

Leaders:

_____
_____
_____
_____
_____
_____
_____

Yourself:

_____
_____
_____
_____
_____
_____
_____

. . . .

THURSDAY: WORK

After WAKING UP, WORSHIPPING the Lord, and WAITING upon the Lord, it's time to WORK...

"WORK hard so God can approve you. Be a good worker, one who does not need to be ashamed and who correctly explains the word of truth." **2 Timothy 2:15 NLT**

All Things New
Read: **Revelation 21**

Sin entered the picture when our first parents, Adam and Eve, disobeyed God in the Garden of Eden — **Genesis 3**. But because of God's grace, His love cleaned up the mess sin made of the world; our bad choices, our sin, is not only covered by Jesus' blood, it's washed and cleansed as if it never happened (though it did) — **Isaiah 1:18, John 19-20, Revelation 21:1**. Only God can make all things new — **2 Corinthians 5:17, Revelation 21:1, 5**! Only God can restore the years the locust have eaten — **Joel 2:25**. He loves us! He makes beautiful things out of us — **Psalm 103:14**.

As we read in **Revelation 21** we see that there will be a new heaven and a new earth, free from sin, and God will live among His people — **Revelation 21:1-3**. His glory will illuminate the city so much so that the city won't have any need for a sun or a moon — **Revelation 21:23**. Can you picture that? Everlasting light!

There will be no tears, because there will be no sin — **Revelation 21:4**! Another sweet promise. You won't experience any type of pain in heaven. Praise God! For we live in a world filled with people hurting due to rampant sin. A world where people are wondering when their suffering will end. We live in a world needing to know there is hope; so we need to share, "hope has a name and it's Jesus Christ."[2] God has given us His Son to passionately proclaim to this hurting world, His love. The love of our Savior secures us, and our Protector promises to take care of evil in the perfect way; eternal death, separated from

....

Him—**Revelation 21:8**. Today, enjoy the abundant life, knowing there is coming a day when you will experience the joyous pleasure of heaven. Your faith will become sight!

How do people get to heaven? Share verses.

_____
_____
_____
_____
_____

Read **Revelation 21:3**. As Christians wait for the day when they will see God face to face, they walk by faith not by sight—**2 Corinthians 5:7**. Name the scripture verses God gives believers about His constant presence with them.

_____
_____
_____
_____
_____

Read **Revelation 21:8, 27.** Why does God take idolatry and dishonesty seriously? Share a verse.

_____
_____
_____
_____
_____

Read **Galatians 5:19-21** and **1 Corinthians 6:9-10**. Who will not inherit the kingdom of heaven?

_____
_____
_____
_____
_____

. . . .

Read **Revelation 21:10-27.** Why does God give us a very detailed description of the holy city, Jerusalem? Explain.

_____

_____

_____

_____

_____

_____

PRAYER: Thank you Jesus for dying on the cross for my sins and

rising again. You are alive, not dead; and I am so thankful for your

presence and the hope I have in seeing you face to face in heaven!

. . . .

FRIDAY: WITNESS

After WAKING UP, WORSHIPPING the Lord, WAITING upon the Lord, and WORKING, it's time to WITNESS!

> "But you shall receive power when the Holy Spirit has come upon you; and you shall be WITNESSES to Me...to the end of the earth."
> **Acts 1:8 NKJV**

How has God's grace affected your life? Share a verse.

_____
_____
_____
_____
_____
_____

Read **Colossians 3:2 and Ecclesiastes 3:11.** Do you long for heaven? Explain.

_____
_____
_____
_____
_____
_____

Read **Revelation 21:4.** Why does this verse encourage you?

_____
_____
_____
_____
_____
_____

Read **Revelation 21:8, 27; Proverbs 6:19;** and **Jeremiah 9:3, 5.** God is a God of Truth, so He will reveal and judge all those who lie and deceive. How does God expose liars and deceivers?

. . . .

_____
_____
_____
_____
_____
_____

Do you struggle with lying? To your parents, family, teachers, church leaders, or friends? What do you need to do?

_____
_____
_____
_____
_____

Read **Revelation 21:8** and **James 5:19-20.** Knowing how high the stakes are, do you know someone whose soul is in jeopardy of facing eternal death? What are you going to do?

_____
_____
_____
_____
_____

Write your prayer:

_____
_____
_____
_____
_____

· · · · · · · · · · ·

REVELATION
the End

. . . .

Week 28: **Revelation 22**

. . . .

MONDAY: WAKE UP

"WAKE UP, for the coming of our salvation is nearer now than when we first believed." **Romans 13:11 NLT**

Lord, please open my eyes to Your heart. Illuminate Your truths to me.

Speak Lord, Your servant listens.

Read: **Revelation 22**

What does the verse say?

_____
_____
_____
_____
_____
_____

What is the lesson?

_____
_____
_____
_____
_____
_____

What is God telling you?

_____
_____
_____
_____

. . . .

REVELATION
the End

What is your commitment?

_____

....

TUESDAY: WORSHIP

After WAKING UP, it's time to WORSHIP...

"But the hour is coming, and is now here, when the true worshippers will WORSHIP the Father in spirit and truth, for the Father is seeking such people to worship him." **John 4:23 ESV**

My Savior First of All
Fanny Crosby, 1891

When my life-work is ended, and I cross the swelling tide,
When the bright and glorious morning I shall see;
I shall know my Redeemer when I reach the other side,
And His smile will be the first to welcome me.

Oh, the soul-thrilling rapture when I view His blessed face,
And the luster of His kindly beaming eye;
How my full heart will praise Him for the mercy, love, and grace,
That prepare for me a mansion in the sky.

Oh, the dear ones in glory, how they beckon me to come,
And our parting at the river I recall;
To the sweet vales of Eden they will sing my welcome home;
But I long to meet my Savior first of all.

Through the gates to the city in a robe of spotless white,
He will lead me where no tears will ever fall;
In the glad song of ages I shall mingle with delight;
But I long to meet my Savior first of all.

Chorus:
I shall know Him, I shall know Him,
And redeemed by His side I shall stand,
I shall know Him, I shall know Him
By the print of the nails in His hand.

....

What do you think it will be like, standing face to face with Jesus Christ in heaven?

_____
_____
_____
_____
_____
_____

When you worship Jesus, do you imagine being face to face with Him?

_____
_____
_____
_____
_____

When you are around a lot of people, are you able to worship God freely or are you distracted or scared to worship openly? Explain.

_____
_____
_____
_____
_____

What is **Psalm 17:15**? Explain.

_____
_____
_____
_____
_____

Write your prayer:

_____
_____
_____
_____

. . . .

WEDNESDAY: WAIT

After WAKING UP, WORSHIPPING, it's time to WAIT upon the Lord…

"But those who WAIT on the LORD shall renew their strength; they shall mount up with wings like eagles, they shall run and not be weary, they shall walk and not faint." **Isaiah 40:31 NKJV**

READ: **Proverbs 11:30**
Pray for your:

Family:

_____
_____
_____
_____
_____
_____

Friends:

_____
_____
_____
_____
_____
_____

Community Group:

_____
_____
_____
_____
_____
_____

. . . .

REVELATION

the End

Church:

_____
_____
_____
_____
_____
_____
_____

Nation:

_____
_____
_____
_____
_____
_____

Leaders:

_____
_____
_____
_____
_____
_____

Yourself:

_____
_____
_____
_____
_____
_____

. . . .

THURSDAY: WORK

After WAKING UP, WORSHIPPING the Lord, and WAITING upon the Lord it's time to WORK...

"WORK hard so God can approve you. Be a good worker, one who does not need to be ashamed and who correctly explains the word of truth." **2 Timothy 2:15 NLT**

Home
Read **Revelation 22**

We are sojourners, walking through this life on earth for a season, taking steps toward heaven every day — **1 Peter 1:17**. As we walk in the fear of the Lord we know this life is not empty, but abundant, because God paid a ransom for our sin, with the precious life-blood of Jesus Christ — **1 Peter 1:18-19**; assuring us eternal life in heaven – home with Him.

In **Revelation 22**, the angel showed John a pure river of water of life, flowing from the throne of God and the Lamb; signifying eternal life in God's presence. The tree of life grew on each side of the river, bearing twelve fruits, with fresh fruit born each month; with healing in its leaves, curing the nations. See, the tree of life symbolizes eternal life and the abundance found in eternal life. In heaven we will continue to learn[3] and our continual growth in our knowledge of God will feed our soul, healing us with complete understanding. But know this, we will only experience the abundance found in heaven's eternity because of our relationship with Jesus Christ, for glorious riches are given to us in Christ alone — **John 17:24, Philippians 4:19**.

Sin can no longer separate God's people from Him and His promised rest, as the curse brought on by the Fall of man in the Garden of Eden was judged with finality by the throne of God — **Revelation 20:11-13**. In heaven, the people will be face to face with God, loving Him with their mind; serving Him with undivided attention — **Revelation 22:3-4**. There is no night and no need for a lamp or sun; as the Lord God is

....

their eternal light, shining on them — **Revelation 22:5**. And there the people will reign forever and ever, accepted in the Beloved — **Revelation 22:5; Ephesians 1:3-11**.

In **Revelation 22:6 NKJV**, the angel told John, "These words are faithful and true." Everything John had heard and seen and was told to write were true; out of His love for His people, the Lord God sent His angel to show His servants what will happen — **Revelation 22:6b; 1:1**. The time is near for its fruition, and in this the people witness how God's mercy endures forever — **Psalm 136**. God is so faithful and compassionate towards His people - He not only warns of the coming judgement for all who refuse to believe in Jesus Christ, but He assures a blessing for all who read and hear the words of this prophecy and obey it's decrees — **Revelation 22:7; 1:3**.

John then begins speaking again and admits that when he saw and heard these things spoken by the angel he fell down to worship before the feet of the angel — **Revelation 22:8**. The angel corrected him immediately in **Revelation 22:9 NLT**, saying, "No, don't worship me. I am a servant of God, just like you and your brothers the prophets, as well as all who obey what is written in this book. Worship only God!"

After this, John shares Jesus' words to the church, "And behold, I am coming quickly, and My reward is with Me, to give to every one according to his work. I am the Alpha and the Omega, the Beginning and the End, the First and the Last" — **Revelation 22:12-13 NKJV**. All those who accepted Jesus Christ as their Lord and Savior, cleansed by the blood of the Lamb, forgiven of sin, and sanctified by His teaching that purifies a heart - access the tree of life, entering the gates into the city, beholding the glory of the Lord — **Revelation 22:14; John 17:17, 19, 24**.

Read **Revelation 22:20**. Jesus says He is coming soon. As believers wait for Jesus to come, what does God say is required of them? Read **2 Peter 3:11-18**.

_____

_____

_____

_____

_____

. . . .

What does the Bible say about heaven? Read **Genesis 1:1, 2 Corinthians 5:1, Psalm 11:4, Jeremiah 31:37,** and **Revelation 7:16-17.**

Write out **1 Thessalonians 5:9-10.** Memorize it and share with a friend.

PRAYER: Amen. Even so, come, Lord Jesus!

FRIDAY: WITNESS

After WAKING UP, WORSHIPPING the Lord, WAITING upon the Lord, and WORKING, it's time to WITNESS!

> "But you shall receive power when the Holy Spirit has come upon you; and you shall be WITNESSES to Me...to the end of the earth."
> **Acts 1:8 NKJV**

Read **2 Peter 3:14.** Are you at peace with God?

_____
_____
_____
_____
_____
_____

Read **Revelation 22:12.** People remember the smallest acts of kindness, as does our Lord — **Matthew 10:42**. Knowing Jesus Christ is coming back soon, what legacy are you leaving?

_____
_____
_____
_____
_____
_____

Read **2 Timothy 1:6-7.** God has given you gifts to use for His glory while you are here on earth! Fill in the blank:

God chose me to be _____ ,
_____ , and
_____ .

The book of **Revelation** reveals Jesus Christ!
After reading the book of **Revelation:**

Read **1 Peter 3:15.** Are you prepared to answer questions about the

. . . .

end times? About Jesus? Explain.

_____
_____
_____
_____
_____
_____

What did you learn about Jesus?

_____
_____
_____
_____
_____
_____

How do you desire to live, knowing what will happen in the future?

_____
_____
_____
_____
_____
_____

How has your heart changed toward those that do not know Jesus?

_____
_____
_____
_____
_____
_____

Are you saying, "Amen. Even so, come, Lord Jesus!" **Revelation 22:20**

_____
_____
_____
_____
_____
_____

. . . .

REVELATION
the End

If you were to summarize the book, to share with your family or friends, what would you say?

_____

_____

_____

_____

_____

_____

PRAYER: Abba! My soul delights in Jesus Christ and the abundant life You give. Thank You for Your Sovereign protection and for Your promise of Jesus' coming and the abundance in heaven.

. . . .

Bibliography

Bonhoeffer, D. (1995). *The Cost of Discipleship*. New York, NY: Simon & Schuster.

Courson, J. (2003). *Jon Courson's Application Commentary: New Testament*. Nashville, TN: Thomas Nelson.

Graham-Lotz, A. (2009). *The Vision of His Glory*. Nashville, TN: Thomas Nelson.

Lasseigne, J. (2011). *Unlocking the Last Days: A Guide to the Book of Revelation & the End Times*. Grand Rapids, MI: Baker Books.

Laurie, G. (2014). *Revelation: The Next Dimension*. Austin, TX: Kerygma Publishing.

MacArthur, J. (1999). *The MacArthur New Testament Commentary: Revelation 1-11*. Chicago, IL: Moody Publishers.

MacArthur, J. (1999). *The MacArthur New Testament Commentary: Revelation 12-22*. Chicago, IL: Moody Publishers.

Notes

[i] Anne Graham Lotz has a devotional guide in her book, *The Vision of His Glory.* I used her steps to reading God's Word as a guide, but adjusted them to fit the youth.

[1] Anne Graham Lotz, *The Vision of His Glory.*

[2] Dietrich Bonhoeffer, *The Cost of Discipleship.*

[3] Pastor Greg Laurie, April 21, 2019, a Sunday service, retrieve from www.harvest.org. Pastor Greg made the point that we will continue to learn in heaven.

Made in the USA
Monee, IL
26 March 2024

55805312R00197